Aging, Politics, and Research

BETTY A. LOCKETT is Regional Advisor for Human Resources Planning with the Pan American Health Organization, Regional Office of the World Health Organization in Washington, D.C. Dr. Lockett is a political scientist and educator who has served as a health policy analyst and as chief of the office of International Programs at the National Institutes of Health and the Health Resources Administration of the U.S. Department of Health and Human Services. In 1975 she received the Health Resources Administration Special Achievement award for outstanding leadership, and in 1976 was selected by the U.S. Civil Service Commission for its Executive Development Program.

As a scholar with the Veterans Administration Scholars Program from 1977 until 1980, Dr. Lockett studied health policy and management problems related to the health of the elderly. This book is based, in part, on her research during that period. Dr. Lockett held appointments as Research Associate at The Johns Hopkins University School of Public Health, as professor at the Amrit Science College in Katmandu, Nepal and at the University of Hawaii, Hilo Campus. She was also a Teaching Fellow at the American University were she received her Ph.D. degree in 1970.

Aging, Politics, and Research

Setting the Federal Agenda
for Research on Aging

Betty A. Lockett, Ph.D.

Springer Publishing Company
New York

Copyright © 1983 by Springer Publishing Company, Inc.

Springer Publishing Company, Inc.
200 Park Avenue South
New York, New York   10003

83 84 85 86 87 / 10 9 8 7 6 5 4 3 2 1

Library of Congress Cataloging in Publication Data

Lockett, Betty A.
  Aging, politics, and research.
  Includes bibliographical references and index.
  1. National Institute on Aging. 2. Aging—Research—Uni-
ted States—History. I. Title. [DNLM: 1. Aged—United
States—Legislation. 2. Aging—United States—Legisla-
tion. 3. Policy making. WT 30 L815a]
HQ1064.U5L62 1983   305.2'6'072073   83-522
ISBN 0-8261-4430-6

Printed in the United States of America

Contents

116959

Foreword

Because government policies and programs are understood to
reflect needs of the times, future generations may wonder
why it was not until 1974 that the United States government
created a National Institute on Aging. Demographic patterns, beginning in the 1950's, clearly showed an increasingly older population in the United States. Patterns of
health care services and costs in the 1960's similarly
suggested the need for new strategies and emphases.
Thousands of individual cases where illness and debilitation
curbed human activity too soon--by contrast with greater
numbers of even older people living healthy and active
existences--could have inspired a concerted effort to
overcome the anomaly, through research, many years sooner.
A requisite scientific base, the touchstone of thoughtful
science administrators and policymakers, would have
justified it and most American voters and taxpayers would
have supported it, as they did when the proposition finally
arrived in the legislative arena.

Yet history shows new instruments of social policy are most
often forged with great difficulty, even though the times
may call for them. Certainly this is the case of the
National Institute on Aging, the most recent component of
that great agency which promotes scientific advances and
the enhancement of life and health--the National Institutes
of Health.

Dr. Betty Lockett, in this book, has chronicled the history
of the creation of the new institute in a way that will
fascinate interested laypersons and teach budding political
scientists, including those getting their training on the
job as well as those learning in the classroom. Her book
is an important addition to political science literature
and to the history of social programs. It enhances the
understanding of the challenge to physicians, scientists,
and policymakers of a major social phenomenon of the latter
part of the twentieth century--the aging of America.

Those who read this book will come to understand the natural
as well as artificial impediments to the establishment of
new bureaus even when needs are clear, costs are relatively
low, and the potential advantages of action would seem to
greatly outweigh the option of doing nothing. This work
is, as well, a dramatization of the persistent possibility--
even in a period when government seems vast, distant, and
impermeable--that individual citizens _can_ persuade those
who hold political power to act on behalf of future
generations, if the case is good and the cause is right.

Stephen P. Strickland, Ph.D.
Vice-President
Aspen Institute
Washington, D.C.

Preface

The events, circumstances, and forces which have fostered and opposed support for research on aging for over forty years are traced in this book. The push for aging research became a demand for a separate institute for research on aging in the early 1960's and culminated in 1974 as legislation to create the National Institute on Aging (NIA).

The scope of this book is limited to research on the aging process and does not trace research related to the delivery of health and social services for the elderly conducted by numerous federal agencies. The federal agency of focus is therefore the National Institutes of Health, with mention of related research conducted at the National Institute of Mental Health and at the Veterans Administration.

As the research for the book progressed, early events began to fall into a pattern of organization relevant to the agenda-setting model. The agenda-setting model is used in political science for analyzing "the process by which demands of various groups in the population are translated into items vying for the serious attention of public officials."[1] This process, called "agenda building," occurs in every political system, whether decision makers act through a Congress or a tribal council. The model is an attempt to account "for variation in the ways issues get on the agenda and in rates of success at achieving agenda status," and for "strategies used to prevent the success of

initiating groups."[2] The agenda-setting model is still
evolving, but the publications about this theoretical
approach are adequate to establish it as a credible and
significant concept.[3]

Use of the agenda-setting model as a framework for tracking
the events leading to the establishment of the National
Institute on Aging provides two advantages. First, the
model is a structural means of describing patterns of human
behavior and political events; though the configurations
of patterns may be almost limitless, some patterns are
repeated more often than others. In this study of the NIA
agenda item, the model was not used as a tool to predeter-
mine or eliminate events or research materials, but as a
context for organizing and analyzing information. Second,
the model is a basis for inference about mobilization of
democratic forces to achieve social change and political
action in other policy areas. The circumstances and content
of the NIA cases, of course, will not repeat themselves in
the same form in other policy areas; however, a discernible
pattern in the NIA agenda-building process may provide insight into the policy- and decision-making processes for
other issues.

This account of the creation of the National Institute on
Aging is based on examination of congressional committee
hearings, reports, and bills; administrative task force
reports; files of the National Institutes of Health, the
Veterans Administration, and the Office of Management and
Budget; and other published and unpublished primary documents and secondary sources. In addition, more than fifty
semistructured interviews were held with legislative staff
members, congressmen, government officials, lobbyists,
gerontologists, and other scientists and advocates interested in the elderly. Whenever a statement or remembrance
of fact given in an interview could not be documented by a
primary source, an effort was made to establish no less than
two cross-references to verify that incident as fact.

Four books provided the contextual orientation and
inspiration for an analysis of the establishment of the
National Institute on Aging. In his description of the
rise of the National Institutes of Health, Politics,
Science, and Dread Disease, Stephen P. Strickland gives a
historical perspective on the politics of biomedical
research and vivid picture of the "behind the scenes" role
of lobbyists in the policy development process. Richard A.
Rettig's book, Cancer Crusade: The Story of the National

Cancer Act of 1971, not only analyzed the political significance of the interactions among scientific, political, and
public interest groups in producing the National Cancer Act
but also introduced the concept of agenda-building in the
area of biomedical research. Eric Redman's The Dance of
Legislation, by presenting such a readable inside account
of the development of the National Health Service Corps
legislation, made the legislative process exciting and seem
worth telling for the National Institute on Aging. Strickland's more recent book, Research and the Health of
Americans, carefully analyzes the policy process and points
the way toward the development of a more coherent health
policy.

NOTES

1. Roger Cobb, J. K. Ross, and M. H. Ross, "Agenda Building
   as a Comparative Political Process," The American
   Political Science Review, 70 (March 1976): 126. Except
   where otherwise indicated, this discussion of the agenda
   -setting model is based on the article by Cobb and the
   Rosses, especially pp. 126-132.

2. Ibid.

3. The most relevant publications are: Richard A. Rettig,
   Cancer Crusade: The Story of the National Cancer Act
   of 1971 (Princeton, N.J.: Princeton University Press,
   1977); Henry J. Pratt, The Gray Lobby (Chicago: The
   University of Chicago Press, 1974); Roger W. Cobb and
   Charles D. Elder, Participation in American Politics:
   The Dynamics of Agenda-Building (Boston: Allyn and
   Bacon, Inc., 1972); Jack L. Walker, "Performance Gaps,
   Policy Research, and Political Entrepreneurs: Toward a
   Theory of Agenda Setting," Policy Studies Journal, 3
   (Autumn 1974); and Roger Cobb et al. "Agenda Building
   As a Comparative Political Process," American Political
   Science Review, 70 (March 1976).

Acknowledgments

The research necessary for the writing of this book was conducted under the auspices of the Veterans Administration Scholars Program. I am indebted to Dr. Donald L. Custis, chief medical director of the Veterans Administration, and members of the VA Scholars Board of Governance who not only provided me with the opportunity to do the study but also with good counsel on all aspects of my Scholar Program.

Grants from the Commonwealth Fund Foundation, The Josiah Macy Jr. Foundation and the Glenn Foundation for Medical Research made possible the publication of this book. The assistance of Barbara Lynch in the preparation of the final drafts of the manuscript was invaluable as was the excellent typing of Diana Mantilla and Barbara J. Brandau. Ronald Wylie and Janis Feldman assisted in the organization and research of legislative documents.

More than fifty persons were gracious in giving of their time and knowledge in interviews and, at times, of their personal copies of documents related to the history of the National Institute on Aging. Several persons mentioned in the book read portions of the manuscript and verified or questioned information from other sources. Others especially helpful in commenting on early drafts were my VA Scholar colleague, Don Young; Carl Eisdorfer of the Montefiore Hospital and Medical Center; John Beck of the Rand Corporation and the Veterans Administration; Robert Binstock of Brandeis University; Lawrence Brown of the Brookings

Institute; Stephen P. Strickland of the Aspen Institute; George A. Silver of Yale University; and Philip Lee of the University of California, San Francisco, all of whom gave me expert criticism and encouragement to complete the work.

The patience and interest of friends and family sustained me in this effort, and I am grateful to all who helped--especially to my three sons, Michael, Patrick and Christopher Lockett. It is for them that the book is written.

I
Building the Agenda

1
The Issue of an Aging Population

An issue is a conflict between two or more identifiable groups over procedural or substantive matters relating to the distribution of positions or resources.[1]

Although the National Institute on Aging (NIA) is the youngest and one of the smallest institutes within the National Institutes of Health (NIH), many advocates for the elderly perceive it as the great promise of the future. Others, less optimistic about aging research, see the institute with its broad mandate and meager funding as a pacifier for the public and special interest groups--a discouraging example of "symbolic politics" and "dynamics without change."[2]

For over forty years, advocates of biomedical, social, and behavioral research on aging have promoted their cause as one mechanism for addressing concerns about a growing elderly population. Some research on the biomedical and other aspects of aging was being conducted in the early 1940's, but it was not until the 1960's that the multidisciplinary voices of gerontologists and a few other influential persons and groups were heard, placing the issue of aging research on the public agenda of the nation. After fourteen years of specific demands for an institute, the issue entered the formal agenda of Congress and the Research on Aging Act was passed in 1974, authorizing a National Institute on Aging.

RESEARCH ON AGING: AN ISSUE WITHIN AN ISSUE

Why was aging not established as a major area of biomedical
research at an earlier time? Aging is a scientific subject
so nebulous and diffuse that even gerontological researchers
themselves cannot agree on what it is or how it should be
studied. In part, views which persist have precluded seeing
aging as an independent process. Although all people age
and die, aging has not been perceived as a major "killer"
disease. The disease problems of the aged have been typically thought of as heart disease and cancer, among others,
rather than aging itself. Among those who do view aging as
a discrete process, some take it and its degenerative aspects for granted as natural and irreversible; others perceive it as an unnatural, disease process:

> Two conflicting views are held today by students of age-
> ing in man. One considers ageing as an involutionary
> process which operates cumulatively with the passage of
> time and which is revealed in different organ systems as
> inevitable modifications of cells, tissues and fluids;
> the other view interprets the changes found in aged
> organs as due to infections, toxins, traumas, and nutri-
> tional disturbances or inadequacies which have forced
> cells, tissues and fluids to respond with degenerative
> changes and impairments. It appears, however, that at
> least some of these changes serve to maintain function-
> ing and are therefore protective. The issue becomes
> sharply focused upon the possibility of distinguishing
> between the cumulative but physiological involutions
> that inevitably take place in all individuals as they
> grow older, and pathological changes that occur in age-
> ing individuals as the result of adverse environmental
> conditions.[3]

These words come not from a current professional journal,
but from the foreword of a book on scientific research on
the problems of aging, published in 1938 at a time when the
population of the United States was 129 million, half the
population of today. There was no comprehensive and costly
social security system in the United States. Gray power did
not exist, nor was the runaway cost of medical and nursing
home care for the aged a national political issue.[4]

Throughout the ensuing forty years, questions were continually raised about the very nature and definition of aging
research. There was much debate about whether there could
or should be study of the process of aging. Some saw the

problems of the elderly as chiefly psychosocial and often
emphasized the need for services rather than research.
Others viewed the problems as basically economic. As one
elderly physician said, "As long as I have my marbles and
money I'll be fine." Old age is still typically viewed as
inevitable and attempts to promote a longer or even
healthier life during the aging process have met with skepticism and opposition from the established biomedical community. For the most part, medical academicians concerned
with research of disease process and mechanisms have had
little interest in the disablements of the aged and in the
disabilities that affect the elderly due to chronic disease;
efforts to include gerontology and geriatrics in medical
school curricula were rejected until recently. Most biomedical investigators and many laymen felt that if specific
diseases were studied and conquered, the elderly could live
to a healthy old age. Those who would study aging in order
to retard or halt the process have been considered on the
fringe of biomedical research, looking for the fountain of
youth. More importantly, most researchers see few opportunities for scientific investigation in this area.

The debate over aging research continued even as Congress
created the National Institute on Aging. In 1974, Congress
mandated that, "The Secretary...shall...develop a plan for a
research program on aging designed to coordinate and promote
research into the biological, medical, psychological, social, educational, and economic aspects of aging."[5] An
underlying premise of the research plan developed by the
National Institute on Aging in 1977 was that "effective
programs for the aged...must be based on knowing which
changes in the aged are intrinsic to the aging process and
which are not." But first, it is acknowledged that "We do
not know what aging is. Consequently, we cannot crisply
separate the changes--social, behavioral, biological--in-
trinsic to aging, from those changes imposed by medical
history, cultural and ethnic settings, the manner of a
person's life, and other externals."[6] This 1977 statement is an echo of the 1938 scientific dilemma.

How then could a demand for support for a marginal area of
biomedical research with so little backing from the scientific community gain enough momentum to overcome resistance
from the president himself and attain national prominence
in the form of a separate institute at the internationally
prestigious biomedical research center, the National
Institutes of Health?

AGENDA-SETTING AND COALITION BUILDING

An uneasy coalition of a small group of researchers and
leaders from age-based interest groups was able to influence
biomedical research policy and bring about the creation of
the National Institute on Aging in 1974. This success was
due, in part, to the unusual clustering of circumstances,
characters, and catalysts in the early 1970's. Efforts to
obtain support for aging research had begun nearly forty
years before, and the agenda-building process which led to
placing the issue of federal support for aging research on
the formal agenda of the Congress was long and tortuous.
Agenda-building is one way political scientists explain why
some problems become issues while others, often equally
critical, never receive the direct attention of the public
and its leaders. The process involves two agendas, the
public and the formal. The public agenda inlcudes issues
that have a high level of public interest and visibility,
require government action in the view of a sizable proportion of the public, and are the appropriate concern of
government. Demands and issues that are under active and
serious consideration by the government are considered to
be on the formal agenda.

The scientists who, in the process of agenda-setting, initiated the issue of research on aging perceived an unfavorable
bias in the distribution of positions and resources for research. Their early appeals for support to improve the
quality and quantity of aging research got little response.
This small but sufficient coalition proposed and tried various strategies before they made the strategy of a national
institute their ultimate demand. The coalition grew to
include lay and professional groups, congressional committee
members and staffers, and individuals interested not only
in the biomedical, behavioral, and social aspects of aging,
but also in the socioeconomic plight of the elderly themselves. Coalitions on both sides of the issue used multiple
strategies, often uncoordinated and unplanned, in attempts
to influence Congress.

Once the item of an institute for aging had been placed on
the formal agenda of Congress, it took the persistence and
skill of an extremely able lobbyist and of a small group of
determined advocates to hold the attention of Congress
throughout the legislative process and to exert enough influence to make the institute a reality, in spite of strong
opposition from the president, the administration, and the
greater scientific community. The timing and convergence
of important events and circumstances, such as the loss of
strong congressional advocates of biomedical research, the

end of an era of almost unlimited federal support of biomedical research, two White House conferences on Aging, the
growing perception of the elderly as a potential political
force and social issue, a national election, and the Watergate events, influenced the issue career of aging research.
Even after the aging advocates won the legislative battle,
two additional years of effort were required to establish a
free-standing institute with an independent staff and
budget.

An institute has been created, but whether the goal of federal support to improve the quality and quantity of research
on the aging process has been achieved remains a question.
The story of the National Institute on Aging illustrates
the impact that a handful of indiviudals from outside of
government can have on biomedical research policy by working
within the political process. It also reveals how not only
political and social events, but also the very nature of
aging research and the strategies of its advocates and
opponents influence the institute's mandate and future.

NOTES

1. Roger W. Cobb and Charles D. Elder. Participation in
    American Politics: The Dynamics of Agenda-Building
    (Baltimore: Johns Hopkins Press, 1972), p. 82.

2. See Murray Edelman, The Symbolic Uses of Politics
    (Urbana: University of Illinois Press, 1964), for a
    discussion of the importance of symbols in elite
    manipulation of mass political behavior. See also
    Robert R. Alford, Health Care Politics: Ideological
    and Interest Group Barriers to Reform (Chicago:
    University of Chicago Press, 1975) for his thesis
    regarding the inability of interest groups to bring
    about meaningful change in the New York City health
    care system.

3. Lawrence K. Frank, "Foreword," Problems of Ageing:
    Biological and Medical Aspects (Baltimore: The
    Williams and Wilkins Co., 1939), p. xiii.

4. See Robert B. Hudson and Robert H. Binstock, "Political
    Systems and Aging" in Handbook of Aging and the Social
    Sciences (New York: Van Nostrand Reinhold Co., 1976),
    pp. 369-400 for a discussion of the differences between
    the pension reform movements such as the Townsend Move-
    ment and the McLain organization of the 1930's period
    and contemporary aging-based membership organizations.

See also H.J. Pratt, <u>The Gray Lobby</u> (Chicago: University of Chicago Press, 1976). Pratt sees contemporary organizations as part of a larger social movement and in contrast the Townsend and McLain groups as a response to specific problems of the elderly brought about the depression of the 1930's.

5. <u>P.L. 93-296</u>, Section 2, 93rd Congress, May 31, 1974, pp. 2-3.

6. <u>Our Future Selves</u> (Bethesda, Md.: National Institute on Aging, 1977), DHEW Pub. No. 77-1096, pp. 32.

2
Initiation
The Push from the Private Sector

Initiation is the...articulation of a grievance in very
general terms by a group outside the formal government
structure.[1]

During the past forty years, as unprecedented conditions
associated with the increasing proportion of an aging population have ripened, related economic, social, and political
issues have fermented. Those who anticipated the problems
also saw their potential for social disaster by the end of
the century. To avert that perceived social disaster, a
number of forces and events merged during the late 1930's
and the 1940's, partially by historical effect and partially
by chance, to make the need for research on aging a national
issue and to involve all relevant disciplines in that research. In the beginning, the goal to acquire support of
aging research was pursued through established mechanisms--
requests to federal agencies, especially the National Institutes of Health, and to the Congress. However, competitive
interests and opposing forces deterred the realization of
the goal. Eventually, what had been perceived as a need
became a demand, a struggle for the allocation of resources
for research on aging.

The issue of federal support for aging research was initiated in very general terms. At least six events occurred
between 1937 and 1946 which were vehicles for bringing to-

9

gether individuals and organizations who perceived the need
for aging research and who advocated its financial support.
These events occurred in such temporal proximity and chain-
like sequence that together they seem to constitute the
first organized effort to articulate the issue:

> Support for aging research from a private foundation
> Publication of a seminal book on aging research,
>   essentially a survey of the state of the art
> A series of professional conferences on aging research,
>   and consequential interaction among a cadre of
>   researchers from various disciplines interested in
>   the aging field
> Formation of the Club for Research on Ageing
> Organization of the Gerontological Society
> Publication of the Journal of Gerontology

ROLE OF THE MACY FOUNDATION

The first voice formulating the need for research on aging
in a statement influential enough to organize and motivate a
group around the issue was that of the Macy Foundation.[2]
The foundation backed the philosophical statement with
financial support.

Support of medical research by private foundations was not
unusual in the early decades of the twentieth century; on
the contrary, it was accepted, even expected, that private
sector organizations and foundations should support and
constitute the national biomedical research effort. The
Rockefeller and Carnegie Foundations, and the Hooper,
Cushing, Phipps, and Sprague Memorial Institutes were in
1940 among the 63 foundations that contributed most for all
purposes, with medicine receiving more than any other
activity, about 9.5 million dollars.[3] The total budget
of the National Institutes of Health at that time was only
$700,000, and less than one-third of that was awarded in
research grants.[4]

In the 1930's and early 1940's the Macy Foundation became
the supporting force that gave researchers interested in
aging the opportunity to meet, to share and generate ideas,
to organize themselves into a recognizable movement, and to
publish their findings and opinions both for scientific and
lay audiences. In the interest of promoting research on
aging, the foundation sponsored surveys, books, professional
conferences, and research programs in the private and government sectors. The Macy Foundation was a major impetus

behind the other five events that initiated the issue of aging research.

INITIAL GATHERINGS, INITIAL STATEMENTS

A Seminal Book: Statement of Needs and Issues

A book funded by the Macy Foundation on the state of the art in aging research, entitled Problems of Ageing: Biological and Medical Aspects, edited by Edmund V. Cowdry, appeared in 1939.[5] The now classic book is an anthology of scientific reviews of research status and needs. The two major research questions put forth in the Cowdry book in 1939 persist today: how to prolong human life and how to lessen or eliminate the impairments of late life in order to improve its quality.

The 1939 book was inspired by an earlier survey of the problem of arteriosclerosis which summarized existing knowledge on the degenerative changes and aging of blood vessels. Dr. Ludwig Kast, the first president of the Macy Foundation, was not content simply to deplore the general lack of interest in degenerative diseases and the processes of aging. Instead, in preparation for a campaign of re-search he organized a survey of the problem of arteriosclerosis by prominent American and European researchers—among them Edmund V. Cowdry, a professor of cytology at Washington University, St. Louis, Missouri.[6] The foundation invited Cowdry to assist in the preparation and publication of the survey results, a 1933 publication entitled Arteriosclerosis: A Survey of the Problem.[7]

The publication was of interest not only because the foundation and Cowdry would cooperate again a few years later in publishing a volume on aging, but also for the newly gleaned insight into the aging process summarized in the foreword by Kast:

> The belief grew that arteriosclerotic changes are a manifestation of the process of aging—hence unavoidable and beyond human control. This hopeless attitude re-tarded progress in our knowledge of arteriosclerosis more than any other factor until by means of experi-mental methods lesions closely simulating those of human arteriosclerosis were produced in animals. Two observations added emphasis: many persons live to extreme old age without exhibiting serious deteriora-tion of their arteries; on the other hand, although very rare in children, evidence of sclerosis has been

found post mortem in their arteries....If it is true,
as in a large measure it seems to be, that a man is as
old as his arteries, it may turn out quite unexpectedly
that his arteries are as old as their environment makes
them within the limits of their inherent quality....Fur-
ther studies may reveal that the clock, the solar time
piece, and the changes in living tissue, in terms of
capacity to function, are not synchronized by necessity.
The time impress upon an artery may depend on factors
which within limits may be controllable. Biochronometric
studies of aging of tissues may lead to altogether new
views on the great question concerning arteries: What
is age? What is pathology? What part of their transformation is reversible?[8]

Kast was not only pointing out that the aging process was
an entity in itself to be studied; he also was emphasizing
already that degeneration of cells, whether in aging or in
arteriosclerosis, may well be, at least in part, a function
of lifestyle ("as old as their environment makes them") and
not only a function of time.

These early questions about aging led to additional
investigation sponsored by the Macy Foundation. In October
1935, Cowdry wrote to Kast about the broader aspects of the
problems of aging which became apparent during the preparation of the volume on arteriosclerosis. He felt that the
factors involved in growing old had been neglected, but
would be of interest to biologists, physicians, sociologists, and psychologists. He urged that a propitious
beginning might be made by undertaking a similar study of
the problem of aging viewed from many angles. The foundation responded with enthusiasm:

> Here was virgin territory with broad implications for
> many of the biological, medical, and social sciences.
> Here was an opportunity for a foundation to assist in
> the development of a new field of science which, by its
> nature, demanded the integration of data, methods, and
> concepts from many special branches--a coordinated,
> multi-professional approach.[9]

The director of the foundation endorsed Cowdry's suggestion
to conduct a survey on the processes of aging as they occur
throughout the whole body and to select scientists internationally to contribute to the monograph. In June 1937,
these contributors were invited to a two-day conference in
Falmouth, Massachusetts, sponsored jointly by the Union of
American Biological Societies and the National Research
Council and supported by the foundation. Twenty specialists

in botany, genetics, entymology, nutrition, several branches of medical science and practice, psychology, anthropology, vital statistics, and philosophy attended the meeting. The conference and "...opportunity thus afforded for informal discussion and exchange of ideas between these several scientists, each interested in the process of aging but approaching the problem from a different background of concept and method, proved invaluable in the preparation of individual contributions as parts of an integrated whole."[10]

As a result of this second effort, the classic Cowdry book was published. The significance of the 1939 book was that it reviewed medical fields and aging research from the perspective of all body organ systems; in addition, it presented sociological and behavioral concepts related to aging research. Lawrence K. Frank, vice-president of the Macy Foundation, stated that the purpose in publishing the book was to focus "attention upon a problem which has far-reaching scientific and social implications for a society with a rapidly increasing proportion of older men and women....Through such a presentation of interrelated findings and diverse viewpoints, it is hoped to enlist wider interest in a synoptic view of ageing and to further the study of some of the many questions thus revealed."[11] The book was successful in enlisting interest--the 1939 edition was reprinted in 1940 and a second edition appeared in 1942.

Researchers at that time were aware that they had many questions and few answers. The differences of opinion expressed in the book were welcomed and valued as a foreshadowing of progress because they could stimulate further investigation. Prior assumptions were open to doubt. For example, though senescence seemed a natural process, research showed such variation among organisms and so many exceptions to the pattern that "No general theory of ageing, therefore, is at present available and the question of human or mammalian senescence must for the present be regarded as a distinct problem, within the larger biological question."[12] If aging was most rapid during the first few years of life, was the slowdown in late life normal or pathological? The validity of the statistical methods of determining a norm by studying a sample of people of the same age was being questioned because intensive studies "of both animals and children have indicated that individuals grow, develop and mature at different rates and therefore differ widely even at the same chronological age."[13] One contributing researcher asserted that "time produces no effects--events occur in it but not because of it"[14] and is therefore solely a frame

of reference. If not time, then what does influence aging?
New experimental evidence indicated that longevity, vital-
ity, and functional efficiency may be enhanced by adequate
nutrition. Consideration of the impact of environmental,
cultural, social, and psychological influences was gaining
in importance; the effect of heredity was beginning to
lose its dominance in theories. Whether the impairments of
the total body in late life were primary or secondary
effects of changes in body systems was unknown, but it was
considered naive to think in terms of simple cause-and-
effect relationships. A broader conceptual picture was
being sought for aging. Inspired by the "field" concept in
embryology (a term borrowed from physics), Frank suggested
thinking of the functioning organism as a field "in which
the totality of the parts are dynamically interrelated and
therefore are continuously reacting to each other and to
the environment."[15]

John Dewey wrote the introduction to Cowdry's book and
pointed out some of the social and political issues that
could be inferred about the future from the progress
already seen in the lengthening life expectancy of the
population. In the United States, the distribution of the
population by age was no longer shaped like a pyramid, but
more like an egg cut off at the base. A declining birth
rate, better medical care, control of infectious diseases,
and more adequate nutrition were factors Dewey cited as
contributing to "an unprecedented situation. Over one-third
of the total population will soon be over fifty years of
age. In 1980 the number of persons over sixty-five will be
more than double that today."[16]

Dewey's statement was made in 1938 when the nation's
population was 129 million. The major significance of the
population shift was in its emerging economic and political
repercussions that would require new social standards and
ideals. Issues of old-age pensions, social security, legal
restrictions on child labor, and legal rights of
individuals on the basis of age were emerging as dominant
themes at that time. Dewey emphasized that the many
perplexing problems attendant on old age constitute a
veritable

> ...problem and one of a scope having no precedent in
> human history. Biological processes are at the roots
> of the problems and of the methods of solving them, but
> the biological processes take place in economic,
> political and cultural contexts. They are inextricably

interwoven with these contexts so that one reacts upon the other in all sorts of intricate ways. We need to know the ways in which social contexts react back into biological processes as well as to know the ways in which the biological processes condition social life.[17]

The common ground of science and philosophy in the field of aging was recognized by Dewey and the early group of researchers who began organizing themselves around the problem of aging. Perhaps considered an enlightened viewpoint today, it was a natural approach in the beginnings, in the 1930's. The slow development of aging research in the United States perhaps reflects Dewey's warning that "Recognition of the seriousness of the problem as well as application of the knowledge that is already in our possession is impeded by traditional ideas, intellectual habits and institutional customs."[18]

A 1977 government publication stating the research plan of the newly founded National Institute of Aging, prepared with the advice of the National Advisory Council on Aging, ironically reads like an echo--almost an unacknowledged paraphrasing--of the articulate writing of John Dewey and others four decades earlier. One difference is in the tense of the verb--instead of warning of the imminent social and personal tragedies of a population with an increasing proportion of elderly people, it laments a situation already upon us, and somewhat naively implies that it was inevitable:

> Our social, economic, health, research, and other vital institutions and arrangements were not prepared for the "demographic revolution"--the dramatically rising numbers of people, and especially older people that came with the twentieth century. Thus, the human triumph marked by increasing life expectancy contained potential and actual tragedies for all too many older people and their families.[19]

Conference on Aging Research: Multidisciplinary Interaction

The usefulness of informal conferences where questions could be raised and participants could speak freely became evident during the survey of the problem of arteriosclerosis. When the Macy Foundation cosponsored the 1937 conference on

aging, a definite beginning was made in the organization of
a research group on aging. On February 4, 1938, the
National Research Council's Committee on the Biological
Processes of Ageing met in Washington, D.C. Other smaller
meetings on aging of the nervous and endocrine systems were
likewise sponsored by the Macy Foundation.

By 1940 other influential organizations were holding
conferences on aging: The American Orthopsychiatric
Association, the Medical Clinics of North America, The
American Chemical Society. The next year the Macy Foundation gave a grant to the Public Health Service (NIH) to
conduct a conference on Mental Health in Later Maturity.
Surgeon General Thomas Parran opened the 1941 NIH-Macy
Conference with observations that reiterate the research
and sociological problems introduced in the Cowdry book and
which intertwine the themes of preservation of health in
the aged and the well-being of the nation. With Parran's
words, the research problems take on the stature of an
issue presented by the Surgeon General of the Public Health
Service, worthy of recognition and effort by the federal
agency responsible for preventing disasters in the realm of
health:

> The aged are people whereas aging is a process.
> However, in order to solve the urgent clinical and
> sociologic problems introduced by the greatly
> increasing numbers of older people in the country, we
> need to know more of the processes and the consequences
> of aging....Without health, the increasing millions
> past the meridian represent a potential disastrous
> economic and social menace to the commonwealth. Thus
> the maintenance of mental and physical health into true
> senility is an objective worthy of our most
> conscientious and extensive efforts....
>
> Senescence is not a disease, nor is it all decline.
> Some functional capacities increase with the years as
> others diminish. This is particularly notable with
> certain mental activities. It is thus of the greatest
> importance that far more precise information as to the
> changes in mental capacities which occur with aging
> become available if we are to employ wisely and utilize
> the vast reservoir of elderly persons only too anxious
> to be of use. There is no greater tragedy for the aged
> than the unnecessary sense of uselessness which society
> now imposes upon them prematurely.[20]

For some time thereafter, the Macy Foundation sponsored
meetings annually and published proceedings of those
meetings.

THE SIGNIFICANT CADRE

The Club for Research on Ageing

Around almost any special interest there will eventually gravitate a few people who are motivated to communicate their interests and concerns, to find others who share like interests, to meet occasionally to keep their interests activated, and maybe to meet often enough to plan events or to develop a network whereby others become involved with their ideas. The first few meetings of such a group are usually for exchange of ideas and mutual support in the spirit of their undertakings. Development of the Cowdry book on aging was an important catalyst of such a purpose and process.

Communications and travel over long and even short distances were not taken for granted during the 1930's, the Great Depression. Nevertheless, there did exist a dozen or so researchers around the country who were interested in aging research in addition to their own primary fields of research and practice, and they did manage to identify one another and to meet on occasion. The outcome was the Club for Research on Ageing,[21] organized in 1939, primarily through the efforts of William deB. MacNider, E. Vincent Cowdry, and V. Korenchevsky.

Early during the summer of 1939, Dr. Korenchevsky of the Lister Institute of Preventive Medicine in Oxford, England, visited the United States and conferred with most of the participants in the Macy Conferences on Aging:

> The stimulus given by Dr. Korenchevsky resulted in another two-day conference in 1940 sponsored by the Foundation. Twenty-two distinguished scientists interested in various phases of aging, many of them contributors to Dr. Cowdry's volume, met under the chairmanship of Dr. William deB. MacNider of the University of North Carolina Medical School. The group, now designated as the conference on problems of aging [Club for Research on Ageing 1940–1949] has since met annually in informal two-day round table discussions under the auspices of the Foundation. These conferences have had a catalytic effect upon both research and interest in this important field.[22]

He encouraged the researchers to form a club and establish relationships with similar organizations in other countries. Chiefly because of his efforts, there were nineteen such gerontological groups in fifteen countries by 1949. The Nuffield Trust in England had played much the same role in supporting the British group as had the Macy Foundation in the United States.[23]

In the United States, the club was multidisciplinary, with outstanding researchers in fields other than gerontology, and they were aware that support for aging research was not strong in the biomedical field:

> At the recurring annual meetings of the "Club" not only the progress made but also the handicaps to progress are discussed. It is remarked, however, that enthusiasm generated at the meetings is not shared by others; on returning home members are not met by a starry-eyed lot of young people who want to dedicate their lives to research on aging. The demand for money to finance well conceived research projects on aging remains somewhat disappointing...however, the volume of research on aging is probably greater than it appears to be at the first glance, because it is spread thin in so many fields of activity. The encouraging fact often remarked upon is the wholehearted recognition of the importance of these problems in the fields of sociology and economics and the important investigations already under way therein.[24]

The importance of such a group increases as the group becomes larger and better organized; they become not only a focus for the field, but also promoters of it. By 1945 there were twenty-four members in the Club for Research on Ageing and the club had sponsored fifteen conferences, all supported by the Macy Foundation. The group appointed a committee in 1944 to explore the possibility of starting a publication in the field of gerontology, a sign of their expanding viewpoint and desire to promote aging research.

The Gerontological Society: Organization with a Message

At a meeting of the Club for Research on Ageing on February 10, 1945, the members voted to incorporate the club as a nonprofit organization. On May 8 the name "Gerontological Society" was adopted and the Certificate of Incorporation was signed. Officers were elected at the first meeting of the Gerontological Society on June 14, 1945, in New York City: W. deB. MacNider, president; R. A. Moore, treasurer; and E. J. Stieglitz, secretary. The first members and officers of the new society were all in biological and medical fields even though the society itself was to encompass all other disciplines concerned with aging. The stated purposes of the society clearly demonstrated a multi-disciplinary approach to clinical and basic research:

...to promote the scientific study of aging, in order to advance public health and mental hygiene, the science and art of medicine, and the cure of diseases; to foster the growth and diffusion of knowledge relating to problems of aging and of the sciences contributing to an understanding thereof; to afford a common meeting ground for representation of the various scientific fields interested in such problems and those responsible for care and treatment of the aged; all without profit to the corporation or its members.[25]

One of the first activities of the society was to establish a Registry of Gerontology at the Surgeon General's museum in Washington, D.C., a result of a decision by the Club for Research on Ageing to cooperate in setting up a repository for tissues obtained at autopsy of aged human beings. The society received a grant from the Macy Foundation for the Registry.

At that time, though the founders of the society were cognizant of the importance of aging research and were actively seeking funds to support it, they did not seem aware that they would soon have to compete vigorously for a share in the distribution of research dollars. Furthermore, they apparently believed that scientists could remain detached from political processes and still acquire support, because their charter specifically stated that "No part of the activities of the corporation would attempt to influence legislation by propaganda or otherwise."[26] The charter notwithstanding, the role of the Gerontological Society soon proved to be very political in vying for research dollars when funding sources shifted from private foundations to the federal government.

The Journal of Gerontology

Meanwhile, the club's Publication Committee,[27] which had met on February 9, 1945, reported in April "that life could be discerned" regarding the genesis of a journal and suggested that an editor-in-chief be appointed.[28] It was agreed that the journal would carry articles not only in the biological sciences, but also in medicine, the social sciences, and the humanities. The society sought to appeal to all groups interested in the problems of aging, especially from the economic, sociological, psychological, and medical aspects. Catering to the diversity of interests represented in the society, the editors prepared two addenda to accompany each article: (1) a brief sketch about the author so that clinicians, biologists, sociologists, and so forth, could come to know of one another and (2) an abstract

in nontechnical language so that those in all fields might
clearly understand the work.[29] Furthermore, the society
sought to inform and involve the lay public in issues of
research on aging. A supplement intended for the lay
public was published with each issue of the Journal of
Gerontology. The supplements abridged the articles of the
Journal in nontechnical language. The society was conscious
of the potential for applied research and, therefore, of
the need to communicate the issues of aging to society.
The quotation adopted for the masthead was "To add life to
years, not just years to life."

If a political role for the Gerontological Society was
denied by its charter, its publication did not hesitate to
advocate political and social change and to articulate
issues. The first article in the first issue of the
Journal of Gerontology synthesizes the by then clearly
perceived social and health needs in aging research
approaching the status of a political issue:

> In contrast to our present misuse and neglect of older
> people, we need not only a comprehensive, nation-wide
> policy, but more individual and specific treatment.
>
> For all problems of aging we must have more research,
> more explorations in health care, more guidance for the
> aged; and we must incorporate this knowledge into our
> various organizations and services to protect and
> conserve all members of society.[30]

The article was written by Lawrence K. Frank, a member of
the Committee on Publications for the Journal, and the
organizing editor of the 1939 Cowdry book. He concludes
his article with the following statement of purpose of the
Journal:

> Through gerontology, as a multi-disciplinary enterprise,
> we may demonstrate how the varied resources of
> scientific endeavor and of different professional
> groups may be enlisted in a concerned effort to meet
> one of our major problems. The Journal of Gerontology,
> as the first journal dedicated to this theme, provides
> a medium of communication and of interpretation
> commensurate in scope and purpose with that problem.[31]

The tone continues throughout volume one, and in issue four
of the volume Dr. Frank Hinman makes an appeal and a
prediction:

Because of the progress of medicine, an age of elders
unknown to history has begun, and it is high time for
society to recognize its significance and to inaugurate
an "old age movement" in self defence.[32]

Once again, the cadre, increasing in size, potential, and
multidisciplinary perspective, sought and received financial
aid from the Macy Foundation--for the launching and contin-
uation of the Journal, a total of $24,000 over several
years. The Forest Park Foundation[33] contributed to the
support of the Journal from 1952-1958 in grants totaling
$20,500. The Journal's circulation at the end of the first
year of publication was 933, plus 98 for the nontechnical
supplement.[34]

The Cadre and Continuity

A simple tracing of names, while not indicative of degree
of interest or activity, does identify a group of people
with a common interest and purpose who took the time and
effort to write articles, present papers, and attend
meetings on aging research at a time when such effort and
travel were not common and facile. Furthermore, because
the field of aging was not a popular one in scientific cir-
cles, the group's contributions indicate a bold perspective.
At the time, there was no promise, and little reasonable
hope, of money for such research, but there was a growing
need, recognized early by this cadre of researchers who
provided the energy and stimulus necessary to evoke and
organize interest in the issues of aging.

The cadre can be traced through the following early events:

1. Among the attendees at the June 25-26, 1937, confer-
    ence on aging were 15 contributors to the 1939
    Cowdry book.

2. Seven of the contributors to the 1939 Cowdry book
    attended a February 5, 1938, Conference on Biologi-
    cal Processes of Ageing in Washington, D.C.

3. Eleven[35] of the contributors to the 1939 Cowdry
    book were members of the Club for Research on Ageing
    in 1945 when it became the Gerontological Society.

4. Four of those contributors and founding members be-
    came presidents of the Gerontological Society during
    its first eight years (MacNider, 1945; Frank, 1947;

McCay, 1949; Cowdry, 1953). Two of them (Miles and
Frank) served on the committee for publications
that founded the Journal of Gerontology. Moore, a
Club member and first treasurer of the Gerontolo-
gical Society, became editor-in-chief of the
Journal.

5. Two members of the Club and the Society, Stieglitz
   and Shock, were direct participants as civil ser-
   vants in the single intramural, government-sponsored
   research unit in aging established by NIH in 1940.

6. The first two issues of the Journal had opening
   articles by Frank and Stieglitz giving overviews of
   the fields of gerontology and geriatrics.

For close to a decade, the original cadre pooled efforts in
an attempt to organize thoughts and activities relevant to
research on aging. As a club and professional society,
they institutionalized aging as a research area and
promoted their identity as researchers in aging. They used
conferences and publications as forums for exchanging and
exploring ideas. As a multidisciplinary group, they sought
the answers to the question, What is aging? They knew the
concept of aging lacked clarity of definition, but defining
it was the challenge of the research. From the beginning,
the multidisciplinary approach linked aging to social
issues.

As a nongovernment group, they functioned on funds from a
private foundation. By the end of World War II, however,
the growing cadre had begun to voice strong opinions about
national policy concerning the aged population and were
seeking a share of newly appropriated federal funds for
biomedical research. They began to perceive the
acquisition of funds for aging research as an issue. The
greater the involvement of nongovernment researchers in
seeking government grants, the more their need became a
grievance about the distribution of resources and led up to
a complete initiation of the issue. At the end of the war,
an organized national effort by the Public Health Service
for biomedical research was well under way; but, though the
social and cultural issues related to aging were becoming
more prominent, and though money for biomedical research
was being made available, the traditional thinking Dewey
had warned about in 1939 posed a barricade to the
researchers in aging. They would meet with continual
resistance from the scientific community in established
disciplines.

NOTES

1. Roger Cobb, J.-K. Ross, and M. H. Ross, "Agenda Build-
    ing as a Comparative Political Process," The American
    Political Science Review, 70 (March 1976): 128.

2. Josiah Macy, Jr., a Quaker born in New York City in
    1838, died in 1875 at age 37 from typhoid fever. In
    1930 his daughter, Kate Macy Ladd, established the
    Josiah Macy, Jr. Foundation in his memory:

    > It is my desire that the Foundation...should
    > primarily devote its interests to the fundamental
    > aspects of health, of sickness, and of methods for
    > the relief of suffering; in particular to such
    > special problems in medical science, medical arts,
    > and medical education as require for their
    > solution studies and efforts in correlated fields
    > as well such as biology and the social sciences.

    Kate Macy Ladd, letter (April 24, 1930), in Annual Re-
    port for the Year 1977 (New York: Josiah Macy, Jr.
    Foundation, 1978), p. 11.

3. Richard H. Shryock, American Medical Research (New
    York: Commonwealth Fund, 1947), p. 101, in Stephen P.
    Strickland, Science, Politics and Dread Disease
    (Cambridge, Mass.: Harvard University Press, 1972),
    p. 6.

4. S. P. Strickland, Science, p. 27.

5. The book was copyrighted in 1938, but publication was
    in 1939.

6. Edmund V. Cowdry, "Preface," Conference on Problems of
    Aging (New York: Josiah Macy, Jr. Foundation, 1949),
    p. 13.

7. Edmund V. Cowdry, ed., Arteriosclerosis: A Survey of
    the Problem (New York: The MacMillan Co., 1933).

8. Ludwig Kast, "Foreword," in Cowdry, Arteriosclerosis,
    pp. v-vi.

9. Macy Foundation Twentieth Anniversary Review, 1950,
    pp. 32-33.

10. Ibid., p. 33.

11. Lawrence K. Frank, "Foreword," in Problems of Ageing: Biological and Medical Aspects, ed. E. V. Cowdry (Baltimore: The Williams and Wilkins Co., 1938), p. xiii.

12. Ibid.

13. Ibid., p. xv.

14. Ibid.

15. Ibid., p. xvi.

16. John Dewey, "Introduction," in Cowdry, Problems of Ageing, p. xx.

17. Ibid., p. xxvi.

18. Ibid.

19. Robert N. Butler, "Preface," Our Future Selves: A Research Plan Toward Understanding Aging (Washington, D.C.: U.S. Department of Health, Education, and Welfare, DHEW Pub. No. 77-1096), p. i.

20. Proceedings of the Conference on Mental Health in Later Maturity, May 23-24, 1941 (Washington, D.C.: Supplement 168 to U.S. Public Health Reports, GPO), p. 2, quoted in "History of Gerontology," Aging: Scientific Perspectives and Social Issues, eds. D. S. Woodruff and J. E. Birren (New York: D. Van Nostrand Co., 1975), p. 23.

21. In the name of the club, "ageing" was spelled with the "e." In 1945, when the Journal of Gerontology was created, the editorial board adopted "aging" for its purposes.

22. Macy Twentieth Anniversary Review, p. 34.

23. Ibid., p. 14.

24. Ibid., pp. 15-16.

25. Marjorie Adler, "History of Gerontological Society, Inc.," Journal of Gerontology, 13 (January 1958): 94.

26. Ibid.

27. Members: Roy G. Hoskins, Lawrence K. Frank, Edward Stieglitz, William deB. MacNider.

28. Lawrence K. Frank, "Current Comment," Journal of Gerontology, 1 (January 1946): 133.

29. Adler, "History," p. 96.

30. Lawrence K. Frank, "Gerontology," Journal of Gerontology, 1 (January 1946): 1.

31. Ibid., pp. 10-11.

32. Frank Hinman, "The Dawn of Gerontology," Journal of Gerontology, 1 (October 1946): 417.

33. The Forest Park Foundation was created in 1939 by Mr. W. H. Sommer, Dr. Leslie Rutherford, and Mr. Howard Kinsey for the purpose of improving the care of the aged. In 1950, the foundation completed a modern institution for the care of the aged and chronically ill in Peoria, Illinois. It has also established an Institute for Rehabilitation which offers services to the total community of Peoria, but has had special interest in the problems of the aging. The foundation has played a role in over-all community organization not only to improve services to the elderly, but to offer opportunity to older people to participate more actively in community life.

34. Adler, "History," pp. 95-100.

35. The eleven contributors were: W. B. Cannon, A. J. Carlson, A. E. Cohn, E. V. Cowdry, William Crocker, E. T. Engle, L. K. Frank, C. M. McCay, William deB. MacNider, W. R. Miles, Jean Oliver.

3
Specification
Demands for Support of Aging Research

Specification. General grievances may be translated
into specific demands in a variety of ways.[1]

If a small group from the private sector promoting research
in aging was united in purpose and multidisciplinary in approach, the government sector was an arena for factionalism
and struggle. In the context of the National Institutes of
Health (NIH), the federal agency dedicated to medical research, aging research would unwittingly be subjected to the
conflicting characteristics of research issues that predomi-
nated in other medical fields: basic versus clinical research, biomedical versus behavioral research, and categorical diseases versus normal life processes. Though the gerontologists themselves were not divided along these lines,
they encountered the conflicts as part of a larger political
machinery. The nature of the conflicts not only created political tensions and funding impasses, but also posed ideological obstacles to the nature of gerontological research.

The nascent fields of gerontology and geriatrics were being
defined as disciplines encompassing all aspects of research,
treatment, and especially prevention. These fields took a
holistic approach to medicine and viewed health in the context of the entire individual. In other words, health and
the prevention and treatment of chronic disease were seen to
involve the entire person in the context of his or her environment, and not merely the immediate organ site affected.

26

Other fields, in the tradition of infectious diseases, took
a categorical disease approach to biomedical research even
for chronic diseases. Although gerontology encompassed the
other fields, they, for the most part, excluded gerontology.

In his article in the first issue of the Journal of Gerontology, L. K. Frank describes the field of gerontology as
follows:

> The conception of a mammalian organism growing, devel-
> oping, and aging through time while undergoing the
> interaction with internal and external environments is
> central to medicine and to gerontology. Both recognize
> that each individual is a highly idiomatic organism-
> personality, with a life experience and all the hopes
> and fears, the memories and expectations that are as
> much a functioning part of the man as his organ systems
> and functional activities.[2]

Edward J. Stieglitz, a practicing physician who would
implement the first and eventually the most significant NIH
intramural program for gerontology research, described
geriatrics in the second issue of the Journal as follows:

> The relationship of geriatrics to the broader science
> of gerontology is extremely intimate. Gerontology is
> divisible into three major divisions: (1) the biology
> of senescence; (2) geriatrics; and (3) the sociologic,
> economic, and cultural problems of an aging popula-
> tion....
>
> From the view point of the practice of medicine geriat-
> rics is not a "specialty" in the usual sense of the
> term....Geriatrics crosses all these various specialized
> fields, with the possible exception of obstetrics.
> Therefore, geriatrics is better described as a point of
> view or an attitude of mind which takes cognizance of
> the processes and consequences of aging.[3]

Stieglitz emphasized the prevention aspect of gerontology,
which, because of its spanning of all specialties, essentially means the maintenance in health of the total person,
a concept not yet in practice in research policy at NIH
though described as a goal by leaders of the Public Health
Service (PHS).

As the scientific community of gerontologists, of necessity,
sought funding from NIH, they became involved in the
competition for research grants to be funded by NIH and

increasingly in the defense of gerontology as a valid field
for biomedical research.   In the NIH arena, the statement of
need for aging research developed into a fully articulated
demand.   Though advocates saw an important role for gerontology, there seemed to be no place for it; though initially
support for aging research seemed likely, it soon seemed
impossible.   The issue articulated by the end of the 1940's
was now advancing to the specification stage when demands
would be made for an established, funded focus for aging
research in the government.   The nature of the early demands
and the emerging issue characteristics are illuminated by
the struggle for survival and visibility of the gerontology
research component at NIH in the 1940's and 1950's.

INTRAMURAL GERONTOLOGY RESEARCH PROGRAM AT NIH

Even before the formation of the Gerontological Society,
the Club for Research on Ageing and the Cowdry book were
significant enough to attract the interest of a foresighted
policymaker, Dr. Thomas Parran, Surgeon General of the
Public Health Service (1936-1948).   Had his leadership in
the PHS continued beyond 1948, a critical time in the
policy development of NIH, the course of aging research
might well have followed an easier route.   As a participant
in the government's activities to assess the health needs
of the nation in the 1930's when the Social Security Act
was on the formal agenda, and with a laudable history of
service in field units of the Public Health Service in the
combat against infectious diseases, Parran brought a
breadth of experience and a depth of insight to the health
research policy that included prevention of disease.[4]

In 1940, Parran attended a meeting of the Club for Research
on Ageing and in 1941 he gave the opening address at the
Conference on Mental Health and Later Maturity.   Dr. Nathan
Shock, currently Scientist Emeritus at the National
Institute of Aging and the Gerontology Research Center,
recalls that at that time Parran and his colleagues
believed that "the new, the great need of the future was
going to be aging...a very foresighted perception at that
stage of the game."[5]   Meanwhile, Parran's close
associate, Dr. Lewis R. Thompson, director of NIH
(1937-1942), was emphasizing the need for research applied
to chronic diseases.   The need identified by the private
sector was now being recognized by the highest levels of
the Public Health Service.

Parran believed that the Public Health Service could in
some way become involved with aging research and even begin
a gerontology research program at NIH, but there were no

funds available for such a research program. In fact, in 1940, when the National Institutes of Health were just five years old, federal funds were available for only a few biomedical research areas. Although the Public Health Service had defined seventy areas needing investigation, most of the public and congressional attention was on cancer research. The National Cancer Act had been passed in 1937. During the war years, medical research turned to a coordinated effort in military-related medicine.

Nevertheless, because of Parran's and Thompson's interest in prevention and treatment of chronic diseases, Parran's insight regarding the need for research on aging and, more importantly, funding from the Macy Foundation, the Public Health Service made a first effort in 1940 to establish a mechanism for conducting research in aging. Parran and Thompson agreed that

> ...the NIH program in aging should be focused on research on human subjects. At that time, the NIH was purely an animal operation; researchers conducted only laboratory experiments. There was no clinical center; they had no program on people. They had no place to conduct studies on people. So now, with aging research, another set of circumstances began to play into it and they looked around for some environment where the program would have access to people.[6]

Stieglitz, then a consultant in gerontology at NIH, wrote the following explanation in a letter dated May 21, 1940, to Dr. John T. King, chief of Medical Service at Baltimore City Hospital:

> I hope that it will interest you to learn that the Institute of Health is just starting a new unit of research—one concerned with the many problems of aging. As yet this unit is but a "one man show" and that is I, but it is hoped and expected that the program will develope [sic] into something worth-while. We shall be concerned with both the fundamental biologic aspects of the mechanisms and the pathogenesis of senescence and with the clinical application and the so-called "degenerative disorders" so common in geriatrics.[7]

This introductory letter began a formal correspondence that led to the establishment of the first NIH-sponsored program for studies of aging. The letter suggests that the clinical material available at the Baltimore City Hospital and Alms House could be the basis for some research arrangement between NIH and the hospital.

During the one year that Stieglitz was at NIH, he conducted
a national survey, funded by the Macy Foundation, of research trends in aging. Responses to the survey revealed
over 300 active or projected research studies pertaining to
the problems of gerontology.[8]

Planning a Gerontology Research Unit

That Baltimore City Hospital was a likely place for a
research laboratory in aging was brought to Stieglitz's
attention at a dinner of the Maryland members of the
American College of Physicians. Dr. Maurice C. Pincoffs,
head of the Departments of Surgery and Tuberculosis at
Baltimore City Hospital, reminded Stieglitz of King's
interest in aging research and of the facilities for the
aged at City Hospital.[9] Stieglitz's letter stating that
NIH was thinking of establishing an extramural unit some-
where for the study of aging came as no surprise to King,
for Pincoffs had, at a previous dinner, mentioned this to
King and suggested that City Hospital might get the
unit.[10]

City Hospital did indeed seem a likely location for two
reasons. First, its facilities offered about 350 hospital
patients, many with cardiovascular disease, renal disease,
and vascular disease of the extremities incidental to age.
In addition, there was an Alms House, or infirmary, where
indigent and ambulatory old people were maintained.[11] The
infirmary housed about 1,000 elderly men who, for the most
part, were able-bodied but had no means of support. Many
of them had been in occupations that were not covered by
the Social Security system at that time. The hospital in
1940 was set on a 400-acre farm which had a large dairy
herd. Most of the elderly people worked daily on the farm.
Such a population was extremely attractive to researchers
wanting to study the aging process.

The second attractive feature about Baltimore City Hospital
was its receptive attitude toward aging research, an
attitude which later would be important in keeping the
research component from being dissolved or relocated on the
Bethesda NIH campus. In 1938-1939 City Hospital had made
efforts to institute some research programs of its own in
the aging field. King and Dr. J. Murray Steele, at the
Hospital of the Rockefeller Institute for Medical Research,
had submitted a proposal for a research project to study
aging, to be conducted in cooperation with the Johns
Hopkins School of Medicine. Steele's proposal refers to
"the recent book edited by Cowdry" as offering evidence
that "the medical profession has at last become aware of

the pressing need for study as well as of the fact that methods for it now exist."[12]   King had succeeded in creating an atmosphere receptive to research on aging at City Hospital, such that Stieglitz's proposal to set up a laboratory was well received by the Advisory Committee:

> I reported to the Advisory Committee of the Baltimore City Hospitals this morning about the conversation with you, and your visit. They are all very keen about the matter, especially such people as Judge Waxter, the Welfare Director; Huntington Williams, Commissioner of Health; and the Deans of the two Medical Schools, University of Maryland and Johns Hopkins. Everybody wants to know what he can do to help along our schemes.[13]

In August 1940, Stieglitz received encouragement from Dr. W. H. Sebrell, Jr., his immediate administrative superior and chief of NIH's Division of physiology, that funds might be obtained for a technician to be assigned to laboratory work at City Hospital.[14] On September 24, 1940, Stieglitz obtained wholehearted approval of the general principles of the plan from Thompson, and the promise of a full-time technician to be assigned to Baltimore City Hospital. In addition, Stieglitz received approval to spend as much time as necessary at City Hospital to further and direct the clinical investigations. During the first week of October, the Advisory Committee of the Baltimore City Hospitals and the Advisory Committee of the Welfare Advisory Board of Baltimore City officially approved the plan. With enthusiasm but also with realistic caution, Stieglitz wrote King:

> Just as soon as we can select a technician from the Civil Service rolls, this half of the team will be all set to blow the whistle. It is impossible to say just when we can get this done, partly because of the intrinsic constitutional inertia of Civil Service procedure and partly because the Army is having first crack at the Civil Service rolls. I am sure that you will agree that it is most important to be cautious in the selection of this technician because so much of the validity of our results depends upon the accuracy and the honesty of that work. Someone with the propensity toward "sink tests" could certainly put us in a very embarrassing position scientifically. You will realize that I have also in mind the fact that this technician will have to work with a minimun of supervision.[15]

Active, interested, and responsive persons and institutions may be prerequisites for initiating a cooperative research program, but money is required to implement one. Just as no

facilities were available at NIH to study people, neither
were funds available through NIH for gerontological
research. Once again, the Macy Foundation came through
with a grant, this time for NIH and City Hospital to
establish its project in gerontological research. For a
private organization to financially sponsor government
research was not unusual at that time; the government's
move away from private support occurred later, when it was
feared that the interests behind research dollars could
direct the nature of the research itself.

In November 1940, NIH announced the organization of the new
unit for research related to the problems of aging: "(1)
The biology of senescence as a process, (2) the human
clinical problems of aging and of diseases characteristi-
cally associated with advancing years which include the
mental changes of senescence and senectitude as well as the
physical changes...."[16] The announcement noted that
there are socioeconomic problems relating to aging as well,
but stated that the area was not within the scope of the
new unit's inquiry.

The terms of the collaborative agreement were that NIH
would provide funds (supplied for the first year by the
Macy Foundation) for staff and for research equipment and
supplies. City Hospital would provide laboratory and
office space and access to the patient population and the
Alms House population of elderly men; no overhead would be
charged to NIH. A National Advisory Committee with eleven
members was formed to counsel the new unit which relied
solely on Stieglitz. One member of the Advisory Committee,
Lawrence K. Frank of the Macy Foundation, had been in the
early cadre of researchers.

Starting the Section on Gerontology Research

Stieglitz headed the Unit on Gerontology during its first
year, until July 1941. He hired the promised laboratory
technician, Marvin Yengst, who did comparative urinalyses
in the Baltimore laboratory, a study "not really related to
aging research."[17] Stieglitz, who was planning on a
brief appointment with NIH, remained in Bethesda and
completed the survey of aging research. He reentered
private practice in the fall of 1941 and was replaced by
Nathan Shock, Ph.D., associate professor of physiology from
the University of California at Berkeley.

When Shock arrived from California in the fall of 1941 to
establish the center, he virtually had to construct his own
laboratory and laboratory equipment. The United States was

involved in World War II by December of that year and there
simply was no equipment available, though the hospital was
willing to provide any that could be located.   Shock and
Yengst "scrounged around the hospital and the junk shops
and what not and got enough equipment together to actually
start the testing program by the middle of December."[18]
They had only a tiny room in which to build their make-do
equipment and establish their laboratory, but they managed.
They began their studies on age changes in kidney function
of the elderly men housed in the Alms House.

Because of the war, however, little progress was made in
this study area and their attention was diverted, as a
contribution to the war effort, to studying the effects of
vitamins on work output and recovery from fatigue.

Growth and Progress at the End of World War II

After the war, in 1946, the Section on Gerontology could
return to research aimed specifically at determining the
processes of aging, and the forces favorable to biomedical
research before the war were reactivated.   The director of
NIH during those early postwar years (1942-1950), Dr. Rolla
E. Dyer, was supportive of aging research, particularly
clinical research,[19] and the Public Health Service was
seeking to place personnel returning from the war; hence,
assistants and funds were newly available to many research
and service programs.   The first expansion of the Section
on Gerontology was made with five people, two of them
commissioned officers in the Public Health Service.

During the late 1940's, several researchers[20] spent time
at the Section on Gerontology who later became active in
administrative and policy-making positions related to aging
research at NIH and other agencies.   These individuals and
others constituted a second-generation cadre and served as
a transition group in promoting research in gerontology as
an authentic research area belonging to NIH.   Some of them
were active later in the issue career and gave testimony
during the legislative process to establish an institute
for aging research.

Baltimore City Hospital continued to cooperate and provided
more space for research laboratories.   In 1948, the hospital
provided a forty-bed ward for the exclusive use of the
Section on Gerontology.[21]   The remodeled ward was used
for patient studies and for projects involving volunteer
subjects.   The section's medical staff screened all new
admissions to the home for the elderly and gave those that
qualified an opportunity to participate in the studies.

Thus, in the late 1940's, intramural biomedical research in
gerontology was just getting started, and support seemed to
be forthcoming. However, as would become evident soon,
support from NIH in the late 1940's and early 1950's was
more of a chance opportunity than an ideological commitment.

The time was too brief and the times were too short-sighted
for aging research to develop as a fully independent entity,
but there was adequate development for a few years to build
the field into a noticeable and eventually bothersome
structure. In particular, the administrative mechanism
that boosted aging research was its transfer to the National
Heart Institute when it was established in 1948. Although
geographically the Section on Gerontology has always
remained in Baltimore, its organizational designation as
the Gerontology Branch of the National Heart Institute gave
it greater visibility and status. Gerontology research
became a line item in the budget and its administrators had
voice in planning and development. Consequently, for a
brief period, the program, staff, and resources expanded.

Dr. James Watt, director of the National Heart Institute
from 1952 to 1961, was supportive of gerontology research
and has been called the "saviour"[22] of aging research at
NIH during the 1950's. Watt was perhaps an essential
catalyst for extramural aging research at a time when
circumstances were favorable to biomedical research in all
fields.

EXTRAMURAL RESEARCH: A STUDY SECTION FOR GERONTOLOGY

For two decades after the war, NIH enjoyed the Golden Years,
an extraordinary period of public and congressional favor.
Under the leadership of Senator Lister Hill and Congressman
John Fogarty, federal funds for almost all scientifically
acceptable biomedical research initiatives seemed to be
available, especially for cancer and heart disease; yet,
aging research was not carried along with the tide. Soon
after the war, Surgeon General Parran reiterated his
interest in chronic diseases of the elderly:

> New programs should emerge from the blueprint
> state...and all peacetime health services promise to
> gather increased momentum. As the country's health
> workers speed their attack on vital problems,
> particularly those related to chronic disease of old
> age, wide public support may be anticipated. Never
> before has there been such keen and widespread interest
> in health matters throughout the land.[23]

Nevertheless, few other scientists shared Parran's opinion about the importance of studying the aging process as a means of attaining health in old age. They still saw little or no distinction between aging as a process and chronic diseases.

Grant proposals for extramural research funded by NIH were reviewed by Advisory Councils and Special Study Sections, composed of experts in specific research areas. The Special Study Sections had two major responsibilities:

> (1) to review applications for research grants in their respective fields, approving them, suggesting changes or further study, or disapproving them and forwarding their recommendations to the appropriate National Advisory Councils; and (2) as scientific leaders, to survey the status of research in their fields in order to call attention to neglected areas in which research is particularly lacking, and to stimulate the interest of workers competent to undertake needed research.[24]

The review system essentially made extramural funding the responsibility of scientists rather than government.

A Gerontology Study Section was among the first twenty-one study sections at NIH, but the shortest lived. Among its members[25] were the president of the new Gerontological Society (Frank), its secretary (Simms), and its treasurer (Moore), as well as Shock, the principal researcher in the field of aging within NIH. This repeated appearance of individuals probably indicates more than anything the small size of the cadre of biomedical researchers in the field and their effectiveness in dealing with the new system. Also, perhaps of necessity, there was duplication between study section membership and grants recommended by the section. During the first fiscal year of the section's existence, it recommended ten research projects for seven institutions. Two of these grants were to Simms' institution, Columbia University, and Simms himself was the principal investigator for one of the projects. Two were awarded to the Washington University School of Medicine, Moore's home base. Two grants went to Cornell where Clive and McCay worked; McCay was the co-principal investigator for the project. Thus, six of the ten grants recommended by the study section went to members themselves or to their institutions. This again may be an indicator of the paucity of researchers in the field and of the few existing animal colonies available for aging research. From January 1, 1946, to July 1, 1948, the Gerontology Study Section reviewed 43 applications and approved 72% (31), an average percentage for the times among all study sections.

In 1948 the Division of Research Grants reported that only
$242,297 had been awarded in the field of gerontology.   In
August 1948, the Gerontology Study Section projected that
approximately $700,000 would be needed for fiscal year 1950
for research in eight aging topics, and that within five
years (1949-1954) $3.5 million would be needed to study the
entire process of aging.[26]   However, the expectations of
the study section were short lived and the five-year plan
for research was never implemented. The study section was
abolished in 1949.

Views differ about why the study section was abolished.
Shock recalls that the biomedical researchers who were
members of the Gerontological Society had "forced the issue
of a study section because they felt that other study
sections automatically turned down proposals that had the
word 'aging' in the grant application, but that, unfortu-
nately, because there were so few researchers in the field
they were reviewing their own proposals and the study
section was seen as biased."[27]   Others say that not
enough aging research applications were being received to
warrant a separate study section. From 1946 through 1948,
for example, 43 applications were submitted when the average
was 103 and the highest 182.[28]   Others contend that the
section members were "advocates" and were not critical
enough regarding the scientific merit of proposals reviewed.

The Gerontology Study Section was established under the
aegis of Dr. Cassius J. Van Slyke, the first chief of the
newly established Research Grants Office, who was very much
in favor of research in the field of aging. Van Slyke was
later horrified to learn that his successor and friend, Dr.
Ernest M. Allen, had abolished the study section. Allen
recalls that he "almost lost one of the best friends I ever
had" over the dismissal of the Gerontology Study
Section.[29]   Allen's position was that it was not cost
effective to have such a study section because there were
too few applications in the field and those that were
submitted could be reviewed easily by other study sections.
He also felt that the study section "had to be biased"
because they literally were reviewing their own applications
since there were so few researchers in the field. In addition, he raised the often repeated question: What is aging
research?

Van Slyke, who then was director of the Heart Institute,
insisted that a Gerontology Advisory Committee[30] be
organized to succeed the study section. The group never
met and never functioned as a committee; rather, members
of the committee submitted individual opinions on grant
applications related to their field of expertise. The

grant applications for gerontology research were thereafter reviewed by traditional study sections which, according to Dr. Stan Mohler, an NIH staff member at the time, were slanted toward their own disciplines and downgraded gerontology research. The percentage of approvals "went from one extreme to another."[31] The study sections and NIH in general in the 1950's perceived biomedical research as engaged in a war against diseases and did not understand aging as a process, perhaps even a disease itself distinct from heart disease or cancer. The trend of a few years during which gerontologists had been able to have their demands met in the system was turning downward and, as the grievance deepened, more specific demands would be made in other ways. In fact, gerontology sunk to such a low priority at NIH that, according to Mohler, it would have been overlooked or dismissed altogether except for two circumstances: (1) NIH had an excess of funds and (2) Senator Lister Hill (D-ALA) and Representative John Fogarty (D-RI), the two powerful congressional leaders in health, favored research in gerontology.[32]

DEMANDS FOR CENTERS OF FOCUS AND RESEARCH

The treatment that gerontology research received at NIH in the early 1950's and societal conditions in the nation provoked a surge of pressure from external sources for research in aging--from Congress, the Department of Health, Education, and Welfare (HEW), and the Gerontological Society. The problems of the aged and aging were beginning to catch the eye of the public, particularly in communities where large numbers of older people remained and young people had left to seek economic opportunities, and in retirement communities to which large numbers of elderly migrated because of climate or lower cost of living. By the middle of the decade, counties with a higher than average proportion of older people were clustered in New England and the Midwest, where agricultural viability for young people on small farms was diminishing. Likewise, in the Sunbelt, particularly Florida, the older population had become denser than average because of the attractive climate.

Congressman Fogarty was aware of the increasing proportion of older people and the accompanying problems in his state of Rhode Island. He persisted in asking the administration what was being done on behalf of the elderly and, at congressional budget hearings, he kept insisting on programs for the elderly. He was assured that programs were under development, but nothing specific seemed forthcoming.[33] Meanwhile, in 1956 the Senate Committee

on Labor and Public Welfare requested an inventory of
research projects on aging and the aged. The survey
revealed that few federal agencies except the Social
Security Administration had any interest at all in the
field,[34] though top administrators in DHEW were favorably
inclined toward aging research. The Surgeon General of the
Public Health Service, Dr. Leroy E. Burney (1956-1961),
wanted to establish centers on gerontology, and Arthur
Flemming, secretary of HEW (1958-1961), who would later be
a key advocate for the elderly, similarly had a keen
interest in aging research. The Gerontological Society
expressed its opinion that NIH should do more in aging
research.

In short, although few and feeble, specific demands
from the right sources were being made for support of aging
research and they were significant enough for NIH to react
in an impression of support for the field.

A Center for Aging Research: A Paper Organization

Part of the impression of support was the establishment of
a Center for Aging Research on November 27, 1956, as a
focal point for all NIH extramural activities in
gerontology, ostensibly set up to stimulate the development
of new research projects.[35] The official explanation of
the purpose and status of the Center of Aging Research is
explained by its director, G. Halsey Hunt, M.D.:

> Because the study of gerontology cuts across all
> categories and disciplines of science, investigators in
> this field may be found in all of the biologic
> sciences....For the same reason, the appropriations of
> the National Institutes of Health carry no funds
> earmarked for specific support of research in the field
> of gerontology. Applications proposing research in
> this field must compete with all of the other research
> projects being considered at a given series of Study
> Section and Council meetings.

> In 1956, with the concurrence of all of the National
> Advisory Councils, the National Institutes of Health
> began a program of increased emphasis on research in
> aging. Many individual research projects with some
> bearing on aging had of course been supported before
> that time, but, under the new program, a small office,
> the Center for Aging Research, was established with the
> specific responsibility of fostering research in this
> field. In addition, the Councils recommended that the

NIH support a number of university located centers devoted to research and research training in aging.[36]

The following unofficial explanation of the Center for Aging Research, whether more accurate or not, was the working belief among researchers in the field:

> Shannon [Director of NIH], in his testimony before Congress, never would admit that there was such a thing as gerontology and geriatrics. This was the traditional NIH party line. And his approach was always to state that all of NIH is really devoted to the study of aging, because the study of aging means an increase in life expectancy, which means a reduction in disease incidence; NIH focuses on reducing the incidence of disease, ergo NIH is gerontology. And so, whenever a fuss occurred and there were calls from Congressional committees to NIH to ask what was being done in aging research, they'd send a long list of everything from cancer to heart disease. So Congress said that there was no centralization and the programs are scattered all over and there should be a central organizational structure. Well, that's when the so-called Center for Aging Research was established --purely a paper operation.[37]

Hunt characterizes the center as a political maneuver equivalent to the forest fire fighting technique of building a "backfire" to prevent advancing flames from burning any further into the forest.[38] The camouflage of the center seems to have derived to a degree from "turf protecting," a phenomenon readily seen when funds are tight, but difficult to explain during times of plenty. Biomedical scientists and others were apparently afraid that aging would catch the eye of the public and gain public support: "They were worried because not everyone had heart disease or eye problems, but everyone was aging."[39]

The center never amounted to much more than a "paper organization" and it folded after four years. Hunt, its director for two years (1956-1958) and director of the Division of General Medical Services (1958-1962), was a surgeon in the Public Health Service with no background or previous interest in gerontology. The ineffectiveness of the center is nevertheless more attributable to its political situation and organizational charge than to its small, inexperienced staff. As Hunt recalls, "The Center had no budget, no funds, no nothing."[40] It did not even review grant applications. It simply was supposed to "coordinate" what the other institutions were doing in aging research.   To that end, it published a list of all grants related to gerontology research that the other institutes were supporting.[41]

The staff of two physicians did try to "stimulate," or "foster," interest in gerontology research by traveling and interacting with people in the field, encouraging them to submit grant applications.   The second professional staff member (July 1957–July 1961) was Dr. Stanley Mohler, re-cruited by Hunt in San Francisco.   Mohler soon found out that the "Center for Aging Research had no money of its own, but the NIH had more money than it could spend."   After 1958, the full staff consisted of Mohler and one or two secretaries.   Their office space was moved often; at one point he and two secretaries were housed in the attic of the Stone House, formerly a family residence.   Another year they were moved into the animal house for the National Cancer Institute, then down to Bethesda in the Trunnell Building next to a dry-cleaning establishment, about a mile from the NIH campus: "We felt we were not something that was near and dear to the heart of the leadership at NIH."[42]

Mohler believes his talents were not used to the best: "I wrote a lot of speeches for Congressmen on what the federal government was doing to benefit the elderly."[43] When Shannon needed to provide information to Congress on the dollar funding for grants on aging, he would call Mohler personally.   Meanwhile the inquiries from Congress turned out to be more than idle questions or information collection to answer letters of constituents.

Regional Centers for Aging Research and Training

The same pressures that led to the establishment of the Center for Aging Research soon led to an allocation of NIH grant funds to establish five multidisciplinary centers in aging research and training: "It was planned that only a few such centers would be established in various parts of the country, and that a large proportion of research in aging would continue to be carried on as individual projects in many universities, medical schools, and other research institutions."[44]   In addition to creating an atmosphere which would stimulate collaboration and communication among established investigators of various disciplines, the centers were designed to kindle the interest of young investigators in the field of aging, to provide their regions with consultation services on aging, and to be repositories of information on gerontology.[45]

NIH, though not enthusiastic, was obligated to spend money on centers. Aging research advocates both within and outside of NIH recall that "Dr. Shannon was not interested in research on the biology of aging."[46] The grants were funded by several institutes, with the Center for Aging having a vague responsibility for solicitation of grant applications. Mohler was as helpful to aspiring aging researchers as was possible in an advisory capacity, but had no real authority or control of funds.[47]

Despite the enthusiasm at top administrative levels and the generous earmarked funds, the centers never fulfilled the expectations held for them.[48] Burney reportedly was very disheartened by the experience because he found that in these centers designed to be multidisciplinary the medical staff took the lead in research and the amount and quality of interaction among faculties and research groups within the institutions did not improve. The multidisciplinary approach essentially failed. Brotman remembers that "NIH had only a little interest in aging and that its orientation was exclusively biomedical. NIH would not even consider the psychological or social aspects of the biomedical problems."[49] This attitude was no doubt a determinant of the downhill course the centers took. In addition the NIH was permissive toward the centers in allowing them to pursue their own interests, probably a reflection of the belief that gerontology was not a field in itself and that any research topic ultimately is related to aging.[50]

An NIH evaluation of the efforts to develop these multidisciplinary centers summarizes the experience as follows:

> One conclusion to be drawn from the history of the old Centers on Aging is that high mission motivation on the part of NIH and sometimes universities coupled with mediocre scientific competence does not lead to strong centers. When there exists mission orientation, scientific competence, and an approach that is in harmony with the internal logic of the disciplines involved, then success is possible.[51]

Except for the Duke University Regional Center for the Study of Aging, which had a strong multidisciplinary core of professionals dedicated to gerontology and funds from other sources before receiving the NIH grant, none of the NIH centers appeared to have this combination of characteristics for success. Neither did similar aging research centers later created by the Veterans Administration in the mid-1960's seem to have the combination.

Thus, by the end of the 1950's, aging research was "installed" at NIH, but it was far from well established or well
funded.   During these Golden Years, gerontology had only
brief moments of favor, generated by pressures outside of
NIH, specifically from Fogarty and Hill in Congress.   NIH
was reactive to those pressures when it had to be, but even
then tried to satisfy demands with facades such as the Center for Aging Research and the short-lived multidisciplinary
centers.   Though it did not thrive, the Baltimore Center
survived and could be pointed to by NIH as a commitment to
aging research.

NIH leaders and the scientific community still did not view
aging as a bona fide research field, distinct from categorical diseases that afflict the elderly, and gerontologists
produced little to enlighten or convince them.   The small
group of aging researchers was still attempting to define
aging; they had few, clear research leads.   In a sense,
though they were in the infancy of evolving their research
concepts, they were too far ahead of the times in their
research approach.   The multidisciplinary aspects of gerontology studies, especially those relating to social, behavioral, and environmental factors, were not yet a part of
the scientific approach to understanding the causes and
prevention of disease.

By the end of the decade, disappointed by false starts,
gerontologists were becoming disillusioned with following
the established procedures to get funding.   They had tried
to work within the system but had not been taken seriously.
They were becoming frustrated, and would seek stronger
recourse outside of NIH as strategies for survival.

                              NOTES

1.   Roger Cobb, J.-K. Ross, and M. H. Ross, "Agenda
     Building as a Comparative Political Process," The
     American Political Science Review, 70 (March 1976): 128.

2.   Lawrence K. Frank, "Gerontology," Journal of Geron-
     tology, 1 (January 1946): 2.

3.   Edward J. Stieglitz, "Geriatrics," Journal of Geron-
     tology, 1 (April 1946): 1.

4.   In a 1937 speech, Parran said:

          There are sound scientific, social and economic
          reasons for more aggressive attention to the public

health. I think we have reached a stage in our civilization when we must accept as a major premise that citizens should have an equal opportunity for health as an inherent right with the right of liberty and the pursuit of happiness. [Thomas Parran, in Bess Furman, A Profile of the United States Public Health Service, 1789-1948 (Washington, D.C.: GPO, DHEW, NIH, 73-369), p. 397.]

Parran was expressing not only his belief in the need for social services in health care, but also his philosophy that prevention of disease was possible.

5. Nathan Shock, interview, June 22, 1978.

6. Ibid.

7. Edward J. Stieglitz, letter to John T. King, May 21, 1940.

8. Edward J. Stieglitz, Report of a Survey of Active Studies in Gerontology (Bethesda: NIH, Unit on Gerontology, 1942), p. 13.

    Inquiries about studies related to aging are being sent to scientists in the basic sciences as well as to clinical investigators, for much fundamental work upon the processes, mechanisms and consequences of senescence is probably going on in the sciences of botany, zoology, physiology, pharmacology, psychology, etc. (p. 13).

The purposes of the survey were to:

    1) Assist in increasing cooperation between investigators interested in related problems through applying widely divergent disciplines.

    2) Emphasize the urgent need for greatly augmented support to significant studies into the phenomena of senescence.

    3) Stimulate interest, curiosity, and new research endeavors among scientists.

    4) Assist in the formulation of future research programs (p. 60).

9. Stieglitz letter to King, May 21, 1940.

10. John T. King, unpublished draft of an article on the
     history of Baltimore City Hospital, December 7, 1959,
     p. 3.

11. King letter to Stieglitz, May 23, 1940.

12. J. Murray Steele, "The Problem of the Process of
     Ageing," p. 2.

13. King letter to Stieglitz, June 6, 1940.

14. Stieglitz letter to King, August 8, 1940.

15. Stieglitz letter to King, October 8, 1940.

16. Public Health Reports, 55 (November 15, 1940), p. 2099.

17. Shock, telephone conversation, March 22, 1979.

18. Shock, June 1978.

19. Ibid.

20. Dr. Leroy Duncan was on Shock's staff from 1949-1951
     and then moved to a unit that was being set up at the
     PHS Hospital in Baltimore, headed by Luther S. Terry,
     who subsequently became Surgeon General (1961-1965).
     Dr. James Birren, now director of the E.P. Andrus
     Gerontology Center at the University of Southern
     California, was at the Section 1946-1951. In 1951,
     Birren joined the National Institute of Mental Health
     as chief of its new Section on Aging located at the
     University of Chicago from 1951 to 1953. Then, in the
     1950's and early 1960's, Birren worked at NIMH in
     Bethesda where he was joined for one year by Dr. Robert
     Butler who later became the first director of the
     National Institute on Aging. In 1965, Duncan joined
     the NICHD aging extramural program under Birren; he
     became its director when Birren left, and Shock's unit
     was administratively transferred to that unit. Dr.
     Bernard Strehler, of the University of Southern
     California, also worked with Shock and later with the
     Veterans Administration. Dr. William Reichel, editor
     of Clinical Aspects of Aging and president of the
     American Geriatrics Society, also was a Gerontology
     Research Center alumnus.

21. The Gerontology Research Center (Washington, D.C.:
     GPO, Pub. No. 395-667/3010 NIH, August 1969), p. 8.

22. Shock, June 1978.

23. Thomas Parran, Annual Report of the Federal Security Agency (U.S. Public Health Service, 1947), p. 269 in D.C. Swain, "The Rise of a Research Empire: NIH, 1930 to 1950," Science, 138 (December 14, 1962): 1236.

24. Nathan W. Shock, "Activities of the Gerontology Study Section of the United States Public Health Service," Journal of Gerontology, 2 (July 1947): 258.

25. Ibid: Henry S. Simms, chairman; Nathan W. Shock, executive secretary; Max A. Goldzieher, Roy G. Hoskins, Oscar J. Kaplan, Clive M. McCay, Robert A. Moore, Frank Fremont-Smith, Capt. G. B. Tayloe.

26. The section recommended that those funds be allocated for research in 1950 on the following topics:

    1. Effect of diet on longevity and the development of degenerative diseases

    2. Age changes in endocrine function—such as steroid excretion, thyroid function, adrenal cortex

    3. Changes in cellular calcium metabolism with age

    4. Changes in carbohydrate metabolism with age

    5. Age changes in renal function

    6. Effect of age on physiological responses to stress

    7. Fat deposition in arteriosclerosis

    8. Effect of age on enzyme systems of specific organs and tissues

    The topics recommended for the subsequent five years were:

    1. Changes in metabolism with age

    2. Changes in physiological response to stress with age

    3. Psychological changes with age

    4. Changes in work capacity with age

    5. Metabolic and biochemical aspects of arteriosclerosis

From Annual Reports of the Study Sections, unpublished
document of the Division of Research Grants and Fellow-
ships, NIH, August 25, 1948, pp. 37-39.

27. Shock, June 22, 1978.

28. Annual Reports of the Study Sections, p. 37.

29. Ernest M. Allen, telephone interview, June 5, 1979.

30. The members were Henry S. Simms (chairman), Ernest W.
    Burgess, Frank Fremont-Smith, Clive M. McCay, Robert
    A. Moore, Nathan W. Shock, Ephraim Shorr. "The Geron-
    tology Advisory Committee of the National Institutes
    of Health," Journal of Gerontology, 5 (1950): 72.

31. Stanley Mohler, interview, March 11, 1979.

32. Ibid.

33. Herman Brotman, interview, May 15, 1978.

34. Studies of the Aged and Aging, Committee on Labor and
    Public Welfare, United States Senate, November 1956
    (Washington, D.C.: GPO, 1956).

35. The center was administratively under the National
    Heart Institute until November 4, 1958, when it was
    transferred to the new Division of General Medical
    Sciences.

36. G. Halsey Hunt, "Research Grant Program of the National
    Institutes of Health," Geriatrics, 14 (June 1959):
    398, 401.

37. Shock, June 1978.

38. G. Halsey Hunt, interview, June 29, 1978.

39. Mohler, March 11, 1979.

40. Hunt, June 1978.

41. Hunt, Geriatrics, p. 401. Entitled "Activities of the
    National Institutes of Health in the Field of Geron-
    tology," the publication gives the title and brief
    description of each research project considered to be
    directly or secondarily related to aging, 120 and 140,
    respectively.

42. Mohler, March 11, 1979.

43. Ibid. Mohler had completed his medical training in
    1956 at the University of Texas with a specialization
    in aerospace medicine and was researching changes that
    occur in blood during aging.

44. Hunt, Geriatrics, p. 401.

45. G. Halsey Hunt and Stanley R. Mohler, Aging: A Review
    of Research and Training Grants Supported by the
    National Institutes of Health (Washington, D.C.: GPO,
    NIH, December 1958), p. 1.

    The five centers were at Duke University Medical
    School (North Carolina), Albert Einstein College of
    Medicine (New York City), Brown University (Rhode
    Island), Case Western Reserve University (Ohio), and
    University of Miami (Coral Gables, Florida). When the
    Case Western Reserve Center was founded, Flemming
    personally flew out to Ohio to present the check for
    the $2.5 million grant to the president of Case
    Western Reserve.

46. Leroy Duncan, interview, June 26, 1978.

47. Mohler, March 11, 1979.

48. Leroy Duncan, "The Old Aging Center Program of NIH,"
    unpublished NIH document (December 30, 1976).

    All five centers were funded as program projects "but
    because of the special efforts involved in their
    creation these and only these grants were considered
    to be Centers for Aging Research" (p. 1). The
    "special efforts" were no doubt the mandate from
    officials ranking higher than the director of NIH, and
    calling them "Centers" was a means of feigning
    importance and priority. Only the Duke Center ever
    received official designation as a center by NIH.

    The Duke Center, which received substantial funds for
    construction, survives today and still remains multi-
    disciplinary with a strong focus on psychophysio-
    logical studies. It serves as a regional training
    resource, but "has not succeeded in introducing geri-
    atric medicine as a body of knowledge into the medical
    school in general although it is located in the school"
    (p. 2). The Case Western project experienced a rather

curious transformation. The project was originally
multidisciplinary and included a substantial clinical
component. However, "It faired poorly during early
review but survived" (p. 2). The project finally
resulted in a study of connective tissue.

The other projects were not continued. The Brown
University project was a longitudinal, sociological
study of retired people in Rhode Island, Fogarty's
state. Although an enormous amount of data were
collected, the study encountered methodologic problems
typical to most longitudinal studies and the data were
never analyzed. After several brief and futile
renewals, the grant was disapproved because of lack of
scientific merit. The University of Miami project was
almost exclusively biological studies of invertebrates
and rodents; it too was discontinued. The Einstein
project did almost nothing in aging research but used
the grant money to provide the salaries of many
researchers who had other grants from various NIH
institutes. NIH finally disapproved the grant for
lack of relevance.

49. Brotman, May 1978.

50. Shock, June 1978.

51. Duncan, "Center Program," p. 2.

4
Expansion
Creating Interest and Pressure

Expansion. In order to be successful in getting on the formal agenda, outside groups need to create sufficient pressure or interest to attract the attention of decision makers.[1]

During the 1940's and 1950's, the needs, problems, and unfulfilled potentials of the nation's older citizens became an important national issue. The nature, extent, and implications of these problems became clearer and many more Americans became aware of them. Out of this awareness developed a trend of public sentiment, a desire on the part of many people in all parts of the country for action that would solve or alleviate the problems of older people and would help them realize their opportunities more fully.

Social issues related to aging were expanding on a track parallel to the issue of biomedical research on aging. While gerontologists were struggling for funds at NIH during the 1950's, the public and the social scientists were pressuring for national attention to the welfare problems of the elderly. Response to this public sentiment produced national conferences among government officials and culminated in the first White House Conference on Aging in 1961, required by Congress by law (P.L. 85-908). That conference generated the first major public recommendation for a national institute for aging research. Visibility gained at the 1961 conference encouraged researchers to think in terms of new strategies for getting funds.

EARLY FORUMS

A recommendation for the establishment of a National Advisory Council on Gerontology and Geriatrics came in August 1950. The Federal Security Agency (predecessor of the Department of Health, Education, and Welfare) held the first national conference on aging, initiated at the direction of President Truman. The conference, an outgrowth of rising awareness of the magnitude of effort that would be required to meet the growing problems of old people, brought together 816 participants from all parts of the country for three days. The discussion, organized around eleven broad subject areas, essentially constituted an exploratory forum. No action was proposed or taken, but the conferees in each of the eleven sections developed a series of recommendations which became guides for action over the ensuing decade.

The deliberations of the Section on Aging Research led to a general accord about the major importance of aging problems to human welfare, the comprehensiveness of the problems from cell structure to social organization, and the inadequacy of resources for the solution of the manifold explicit problems.[2] The section confirmed that evidence demonstrated the potential benefit to the nation of increased research in gerontology and geriatrics and the need for long-term research support widely distributed throughout the nation. It recommended the establishment of a National Advisory Council on Gerontology and Geriatrics. The early cadre of researchers on aging was still at work.[3]

Attention to the problems of aging continued to increase in the 1950's. In 1952, about fifteen states had committees or commissions on aging. Those states wished to exchange experiences and explore mutual problems, and in September a Conference of State Commissions on Aging and Federal Agencies was held to discuss mutual questions of organization, functions, and services. Thirty states were represented at the conference.

President Eisenhower created the Federal Council on Aging in April 1956 and two months later the new Federal Council on Aging and the Council of State Governments sponsored a national conference on the subjects of coordinating the programs of federal agencies and establishing a central point of contact with state, local, and private organizations. Two hundred and forty delegates attended; forty-one states and two territories were officially represented.[4]

Even though the conference was for state and federal officials, a few members of the aging-research cadre managed to
appear and be heard. Dr. Edmund V. Cowdry again attended
the meeting and this time he was joined by Dr. Edward J.
Stieglitz and a newcomer, Dr. Ewald Busse, then chairman of
the Duke University Council on Gerontology. The theme of
the meeting was individual initiative and maximum freedom
for senior citizens and Stieglitz added his variation by
suggesting that "anticipatory medicine" should be practiced,
that is, anticipation of complications which may arise with
a particular illness and the steps to prevent such complications. His feeling was that people who can be directed
toward partial or complete self-help at the beginning of
their troubles are robbed of that opportunity as they lose
more of their health, initiative, or self-reliance.[5]
Thus, support for aging research, both basic and applied,
was specified at this meeting concerned primarily with
coordination of programs.

Although the 1950 conference was a national conference, it
was not a White House Conference and thus did not have the
prestige or significance of a conference under the aegis of
the president. The 1952 and 1956 meetings were not national
forums but, rather, working sessions for government officials to improve coordination and communication among themselves. In contrast, the White House Conference of 1961 was
a major event in agenda building. At that prestigious,
national forum, a specific public demand for a National
Institute on Aging was made.

A NATIONAL FORUM MANDATED

Congress used its legislative voice to state its concern
about the issues and problems of the aging population.
Spelling out a course of action to be taken by the federal
government and the states, the White House Conference on
Aging Act mandated a nationwide citizens' forum designed to
focus public attention on the problems and potential of
older Americans and to consolidate all the opinions and
recommendations agreed upon at state conferences on aging
that would precede the national conference. One purpose of
the conference was to:

> formulate recommendations for immediate action in im-
> proving and developing programs to permit the country
> to take advantage of the experience and skills of the
> older persons in our population, to create conditions
> which will better enable them to meet their needs, and

to further research on aging....In order to prevent the
additional years of life, given us by our scientific
development and abundant economy, from becoming a pro-
longed period of dying, we must step up research on the
physical, psychological, and sociological factors....[6]

Here was the beginning of the placement of aging issues on
the public agenda in the broadest sense.

Congressman John E. Fogarty introduced the bill for a White
House Conference on Aging in January 1958. Fogarty, who
represented the state of Rhode Island from 1944 until his
death in January 1967, knew that older people had a higher
incidence of health problems and disability arising from
chronic conditions and had long been interested in biomedical research and the fortunes of NIH. A White House
Conference would be an opportunity for him to promote these
concerns. When he presented the bill to Congress, Fogarty
said, "In spite of the many surveys, books, and conferences
on aging the greatest accomplishment to date has been the
output of words."[7]

The congressman's purpose was to spur action by bringing
together bureaucrats, laymen (including older people
themselves), and the best minds working on the problems of
aging so that they could decide what should be done and how
to proceed. The bill provided grants to the states to
collect information about their older populations and to
conduct conferences on aging prior to the national
conference; thus, each state would have the opportunity to
convene its leaders, assess its own needs and resources,
and prepare its recommendations for the national meeting.
Fogarty felt that during the eight years since the first
conference on aging considerable experience had been gained
and many organizations and individuals had become involved
in the issue. He saw great potential in providing an
opportunity for these people to come together and take
stock of "where we are and where we should be going."[8]

The impetus for the first White House Conference came from
the Congress, not from the White House, a reflection of the
administration's typical lack of initiative in this area.
As Congressman Fogarty stated, "It is unusual for Congress
to initiate a White House Conference. I believe, however,
that it was in the public interest to enact legislation
that could create understanding and stimulate action to
meet one of the most serious social developments of our
time..."[9]

Although the report of the White House Conference on Aging
states in the legislative history of Fogarty's bill that

government officials and the Federal Council on Aging testified before the committee with virtually "unanimous support for the proposed conference,"[10] the support within the administration was far from unanimous. The Bureau of the Budget strongly opposed the bill. In a memorandum dated January 21, 1958, an official of the Bureau of the Budget stated that there is "no question in my mind that Budget would strongly oppose. It would be useful to check across the street, informally, so that they get braced for something."[11] Thus, the White House knew that the bureau was opposed. The bureau again expressed opposition to the bill on August 29, 1958, in a memorandum from Reginald G. Conley.[12]

In a report to the Senate Committee, the Bureau of the Budget recommended against enactment of the bill for three reasons. First, the federal government would spend more than $10 billion in fiscal year 1959 for programs for the aged. Second, conferences had been held in recent years and the needs of the aged were well known. Third, a White House Conference would probably not be the best way to stimulate action at local state levels, and the conference could result in developing "heavy pressures for costly new and expanded Federal programs, unless the responsibility of States and communities and of private individuals and organizations is given adequate emphasis."[13]

Nevertheless, in August 1958 the Bureau of the Budget did finally recommend approval of the bill. A letter for the president prepared by the bureau contained the opinions of relevant government agencies, including the Federal Council on Aging. The position of the Department of Health, Education, and Welfare was that it would have preferred a more flexible long-range authority for holding conferences but that it did believe that the White House Conference authorized by the bill could be very useful. However, the department urged that the bill be approved for political reasons: "...the country would be seriously disappointed if this bill were not permitted to become law."[14] The Department of Labor would have preferred a national conference formulated and called through executive action but recommended that the bill be approved. The Housing and Home Finance Agency stated that it saw no need for this legislation and that in view of the present knowledge of the problems of the aging, federal action could best be accomplished by individual agencies and through coordinated efforts of states, localities, and the Federal Council on Aging. The Housing and Home Finance Agency deferred to the Department of Health, Education, and Welfare on other aspects of the bill. The Veterans Administration likewise deferred to HEW. The Department of Commerce did not

object. The Council of Economic Advisors was disposed to
recommend approval, and would recede if the Department of
Health, Education, and Welfare recommended that the bill
should not be signed. Thus, the executive branch was
hardly unanimously in support of the proposed conference.

Congressman Fogarty first proposed that the conference be
held before December 31, 1958; then, in his testimony
before the Committee on Education and Labor, he changed the
date to 1960 to give the states about two years to collect
information, organize conferences, and formulate
recommendations. The committee gave the secretary of
Health, Education, and Welfare rather than the HEW Special
Staff on Aging the statutory responsibility for
administering the act. The Senate later changed the date
to January 1961 and reduced the amount of the state grants
from a maximum of $50,000 to a maximum of $15,000 and a
minimum of $5,000. On September 2, 1958, the White House
Conference Act (P.L. 85-908) was signed by President
Eisenhower; an appropriation of $100,000 was made for
planning to get started.

THE 1961 WHITE HOUSE CONFERENCE

More than 2,500 delegates met in Washington and
participated in this forum for four days, January 9-12,
1961. Two years of preconference work, study, and analysis
by thousands of professionals and lay persons in the states
and communities built the foundation of the conference.
The delegates represented fifty-three states and
territories and more than 300 national voluntary
organizations interested or active in the field of aging.

The basic objectives of the conference were to define the
circumstances, needs, and opportunities of America's older
citizens and to recommend actions by governmental and
private groups that would enable citizens to achieve
maximum satisfaction in their later years. Specifically,
one objective was "stepping up research designed to relieve
old age of its burdens of sickness, mental breakdown, and
social ostracism."[15]

The conference was organized into twenty sections which
included such topics as housing, education, population
trends, and income maintenance. Three sections were
related to research in gerontology: biological research,
medical research, and psychological and social sciences
research. Thus, not only was there a to-be-expected

separation of the behavioral and social sciences from biomedical research groups, but also an unusual separation between biological and medical research. Health appeared in two other sections--income maintenance, which included financing health costs, and health and medical care, including institutional care.

Each of the twenty sections prepared a background statement describing the nature and problems of its topic. The statements noted programs and developments in the field and identified the gaps; they described relevant issues and the obstacles to closing the gaps.

The three sections on aging research all recommended that an institute be established at the National Institutes of Health. The Section on Research in Gerontology: Psychological and Social Sciences recommended that:

> 1. There should be established an Institute of Aging within the National Institutes of Health to stimulate, organize, and support research. This research should include studies of social structure, function, and change as related to health, as well as studies focused on aging individuals. The institute should be adequately staffed with representatives of the biological, psychological and social sciences. In addition, research on social, economic, and political aspects of aging also should be supported by appropriate government agencies. Existing private and public agencies now performing or supporting aging research functions should expand these activities.

> 2. The proposed Institute of Aging should provide for the establishment of regional laboratories which will maintain common facilities for individual research projects, such as:
> a. Making available population samples for longitudinal and cross-sectional studies;
> b. Extending present longitudinal studies in child development to include observations on the aging process; and
> c. Maintaining colonies of pure strains of animals.[16]

The section also recommended that centers for aging research established by NIH should be rapidly expanded, their interdisciplinary nature should be maintained, and support of them from both public and private sources should be encouraged.

The Section on Research on Gerontology: Biological stated
that:

> It is the unanimous opinion of the Biology Section
> that an understanding of the basic biological changes
> underlying the aging process is a proper foundation of
> the applied areas of gerontology. Despite the biolog-
> ical basis of man's infirmities during aging, studies
> on the basic biology of the process have been much
> neglected in the past.[17]

The section traced this neglect to (1) the extraordinary
interdisciplinary bases of the problem, (2) the fact that
specific degenerative diseases associated with aging had
required immediate attempts toward their solution, (3) the
lack of trained personnel in the field because aging
research is not conducted within any single departmental
framework, and (4) lack of sufficient leadership by
government and private research and educational agencies.
The first major policy recommendation of the section was
that a National Institute of Gerontology be established
within the existing framework of NIH to study the basic
biological changes underlying the aging process and other
relevant aspects of the aging problem. In addition, the
section called for the immediate appointment of a study
section on aging within the Division of Research Grants of
NIH. Another major recommendation was that "The Federal
Government should extend its program of support of multidisciplinary aging research centers and programs in basic
biological research in aging. However, this program should
in no way jeopardize the existing support programs of
individual research studies in this area, at such institutions."[18]   This group wanted to see aging research
encouraged in both private and public agencies other than
NIH, for example, the Veterans Administration. This group
also recommended that measures be taken to establish animal
colonies to supply adequate numbers of animals reared and
maintained under standard conditions for use in aging
research.

The Section on Research in Gerontology: Medical recommended
the establishment of an Institute for Research on Aging
within NIH, to include intramural and extramural research.
The recommendation added that the institute should encompass
all health-related aspects of the aging process. The recommendation explained:

> Compelling health problems brought about the creation
> within the U.S. Public Health Service of seven
> disease-oriented institutes and the noncategorical
> Division of General Medical Sciences. These

> governmental components have had a significant impact
> upon the prevention and treatment of disease. In a
> sense, these established Institutes are creating
> heightened geriatric problems, since with each advance
> in therapy a new cohort of aging and aged individuals
> is added to our present sixteen million persons over
> 65. Our knowledge regarding the health of this
> growing segment is insufficient to meet their health
> needs.[19]

The section also recommended that NIH continue to foster
its program supporting large-scale interdisciplinary
research centers in aging. Likewise, they recommended that
the Veterans Administration continue its efforts: "Inasmuch
as the Veterans Administration offers excellent opportunities for research in the geratric sphere, it is recommended
that the present efforts in this regard be strengthened and
expanded."[20] Dr. Harvey Estes, chief of Medical Service
at the Durham, North Carolina, VA Hospital, was a member of
the Medical Section.

Herman Brotman of the Special Staff on Aging was the
technical director for the section on Research on Gerontology: Psychological and Social Sciences. The Special
Staff planned the conference and served as secretariat to
the Federal Council on Aging. Brotman had aided and
abetted the conference bill, as the Bureau of the Budget
noted with displeasure,[21] by helping Congressman Fogarty
and his staff with the bill. Brotman recalls that he and
others of his section had prepared a recommendation which
would have established an Institute on Gerontology in the
Office of the Secretary of HEW and would have combined both
the biomedical and behavioral sciences. As this resolution
was approved by Brotman's planning committee, they met with
Dr. Stanley Mohler and others interested in NIH. Stanley
Mohler from the Center for Aging Research at NIH was the
technical director for both the section on Research in
Gerontology: Biological and the section on Research in
Gerontology: Medical. They debated very late—well into
the morning—until finally they agreed to reword the
recommendation completely and include in the report from
the Section on Research in Gerontology: Psychological and
Social Sciences that the Institute on Gerontology be
located in NIH. Thus, all three sections came out with
very similar recommendations for a multidisciplinary
institute to be located in the National Institutes of
Health.

Mohler's activism at the conference caused him some
problems when he returned to his office at NIH after the
conference. On January 11, 1961, the Washington Evening

Star reported with a headline that scientists were urging
an aging research center in NIH. Mohler recalls that "the
article shook up some of the top NIH administrators who felt
that the proposed institute would threaten their domain. I
took a little heat but it blew over."[22] The article said
that leading research scientists urged the establishment of
an institute of aging research within NIH. Mohler had spo-
ken to the newspaper reporters and said that the institute
was necessary in order to meet the demands caused by a lack
of research in gerontology. He said that such an institute
would probably cost about $20 million, and was quoted as
saying the proposal to create a new institute had met with
the full support of all the scientists present at the
meeting, many of whom held leading posts at NIH and other
leading research institutes.

Thus, by the end of the four-day conference, an active
elite group of professionals from the fields of biology,
medicine, psychology, and the social sciences had come together in a national forum and had articulated a specific
demand for the creation of an institute at NIH devoted to
the study of the problems and process of aging. With this
specification, the issue of an institute for aging research
was placed squarely on the public agenda of the nation.

                        AN INTERIM DECADE

What happened to the agenda item of aging research after
the first White House Conference when it was specified as a
demand for a national institute? Very little. Though the
researchers' demand represented strategic thinking, they
were not organized to act strategically. They were temporarily pacified by other promises, only to become more
frustrated by disappointments.

Soon after the close of the 1961 conference, the Senate
created a Special Committee on Aging, on outgrowth of the
earlier Subcommittee on the Problems of the Aging and the
Aged. As a special committee, it had no authority to report
bills to the floor of the Senate, but was to be a study
group with authority to conduct hearings. It became a useful sounding board for researchers in the 1960's. Though
the original life was to be only one year, the committee's
charter has been renewed each year since 1961.

Considerable progress was made in programs for the elderly.[23] Medicare, designed to meet the acute medical and
hospital care needs of the aged, was enacted in 1965. Also

in 1965 the Heart Disease, Cancer, and Stroke Amendments were passed which had important implications for the elderly. In the same year the Older Americans Act was passed. It set up the Administration on Aging (AoA) dedicated to improving and enriching the lives of the elderly, but its programs were social services, not basic research. Thus, older Americans had their share of the social programs passed in the 1960's, but the area of biomedical research devoted to the aging process continued to be neglected.

Even at the National Institute of Mental Health (NIMH) the aging research picture was not much brighter. According to Dr. Carl Eisdorfer, the spokesman for the Research Committee of the Gerontological Society, less than $1 million was invested in basic research, representing only 3.1% of the NIMH budget. Furthermore, NIMH had only one professional charged with the sole responsibility for the development of programs for the aged, and was "attempting to recruit a 'first rate' psychiatrist into this program at a salary approximately 50% of the contemporary wage scale."[24] The one hope of the decade seemed to be, could have been, the new institute promoted by President John F. Kennedy.

Establishing the National Institute of Child Health and Human Development

The first White House Conference on Aging ended eight days before the inauguration of President John F. Kennedy. Two months before his term as president began, Senator Kennedy had set up a Task Force on Health and Social Security. One of the twelve program recommendations of that group was the creation of an institute at NIH for child health. The announcement of the task force's recommendation for an institute of child health came on the second day of the White House Conference on Aging—perhaps by coincidence, perhaps by design. In any event, it was evident that the health needs of the young would be a priority issue of the new administration.

Apparently, DHEW and NIH did not favor an institute of child health any more than an institute on aging. Secretary of DHEW, Abraham Ribicoff, made it clear that the recommendation of Kennedy's task force was "in no way binding upon this Department."[25] The Office of General Counsel at DHEW provided an opinion on January 30, 1961, that under existing legislative authority NIH could only create new institutes for particular diseases or groups of diseases

and not for the study of the life processes such as child
health, human development, and aging.[26]

In the previous decade pediatricians had not fared much
better at NIH than the gerontologists. Leading pediatricians had been concerned for some time about what they
considered to be the limited representation of pediatricians on NIH study sections and councils and the inadequate
support for child health research from NIH. When they
expressed their concern to Dr. Shannon he reportedly
described pediatricians as "too clinically-oriented to
conduct research of value--'just a bunch of doting grand-
mothers.'"[27]

But the new president of the United States in his first
health message to Congress on February 9, 1961, recommended, in concert with his task force, that a new institute be established at NIH with a Center for Research in
Child Health and that Congress increase appropriations for
the existing health and welfare programs for children.[28]
While the DHEW leadership did not seem "inclined to effectu-
ate the entire program immediately,"[29] the White House
leadership was determined to move parts of the program
immediately toward accomplishment. The president asked for
the comments of both his official and unofficial advisers,
the former primarily from DHEW: "While the White House and
DHEW were simultaneously considering possible actions in
both the fields of child health and aging, the DHEW was
formally invited to react to the proposed National Institute of Child Health. Interestingly, there is no record of
a formal request by the President to DHEW regarding the
aging institute recommended by the latest White House
Conference on Aging."[30] NIH's recommendation to the
Surgeon General of the Public Health Service was to establish an institute concerned with all stages of human
development to be called "The National Institute of Human
Growth and Development" or "The National Institute of Human
Development."[31] The president responded favorably to the
concept, recognizing the increasing pressures in the fields
of aging and child health and the value of an institute
which would incorporate both programs under the umbrella of
"human development." However, he also insisted that "child
health" should appear in the institute's title to assure
that the main subject of the institute's attention would be
obvious to the general public.[32] An early draft (March
1961) of legislative specifications distributed by NIH
proposed two institutes: a National Institute of Child
Health and Human Development and a National Institute of
General Medical Services. The feeling of one NIH official
was penciled in the margin of the draft: "'If we've got to

have this little bastard, this looks as though we are asking
for as much as we can get out of it in exchange for adopting
the little waif!'"[33]

From the beginning of the development of interest in an
Institute of Child Health and Human Development, the
emphasis was on child health and not the other end of the
span of human life. On July 10, 1961, Shannon brought in
twenty-nine consultants representing seventeen professional
organizations to advise the NIH on how it should develop
the legislative specifications, structure the new institute,
and plan its program. The subjects of maturing and aging
were not discussed at this meeting and, more important,
gerontology was not even represented. A memo from the
chief of the Division of General Medical Sciences to the
deputy director of NIH specifically excludes gerontologists
from the list of representatives to be invited to the
planning meeting.[34] Dr. Halsey Hunt recalls that this
was a decision of the director's office primarily because
the immediate problems of program development were in the
field of child health.[35]

Even on the Hill, little attention was given to aging.
Hearings on the proposed Institute of Child Health and Human
Development were held on February 13-14, 1962, but little
comment was made concerning research in aging. Near the
close of the hearings, two witnesses active in aging research spoke, stating their preferences for a separate institute for gerontology. Dr. Robert Havighurst, representing
the Gerontological Society of America and the University of
Chicago Committee on Human Development, stated:

> As I have listened to the hearing today I have been
> impressed with the problem of the committee in writing
> a bill to create an institute which moves from the
> womb to the tomb, and also which covers the whole
> range of scientific study of human behavior and
> development; namely, the biological and medical over
> the psychological, sociological, and anthropological.
>
> I must say that some of my colleagues have been
> dubious that it can be done successfully, and have
> urged that those who are interested especially in
> studies of aging refuse to support this bill. This
> does not mean they would oppose the bill, but they
> would favor, in addition, another institute, an
> Institute of Gerontology.
>
> The White House Conference on Aging of last year
> recommended the establishment of an Institute of

Gerontology among the National Institutes of Health.
My own committee in the Gerontological Society is
somewhat divided on this matter, but the majority of
us believe that it may be possible to establish an
institute which would be concerned with human development from birth throughout the lifespan so that the
research interests of those interested in adulthood
and old age would be satisfied, as well as the research
interests of those who are interested in childhood and
in the period around birth. However, it does seem to
us to be a problem. I am sure that if the proposed
Institute is created, the people especially interested
in the field of adulthood and old age will be waiting
to see whether the Institute effectively serves their
research interests.[36]

The second witness active in aging research was Dr. Ewald
W. Busse of the Duke University School of Medicine, who
indicated that he was appearing as an individual and not
representing any organization. His prepared statement
included the following:

The White House Conference on Aging, professional
organizations, and permanent investigators in gerontology have recommended the establishment of an
Institute of Gerontology within the existing framework
of the National Institutes of Health. H.R. 8398 does
not accomplish this, but it is possible that the new
Institute of Child Health and Human Development will
attain and exceed the hoped-for goals. Only time will
tell. If experience proves otherwise, the situation
will have to be carefully reviewed, and corrective and
alternative measures considered.[37]

Time and experience did not prove to attain the goals of
researchers in aging, but, for the time being, many leaders
in the field of gerontology were content to have aging
included in the scope of the new institute, a seemingly
logical research approach to the developmental process of
the entire human life span.

In August 1962, as the 87th Congress neared the end of its
second session, the bill was brought on the floor of the
House with a proposed committee amendment deleting the
words "or aged persons" from Section 441 of the bill which
read:

SEC. 441. The Surgeon General is authorized, with the
approval of the Secretary, to establish in the Public
Health Service an institute for the conduct and support
of research and training relating to child health,

maternal health, and human development, including research and training in the special health problems and requirement of mothers, children, or aged persons and in the sciences relating to the processes of human growth and development.

Since the committee report clearly identified aging as a function of the proposed Institute of Child Health and Human Development, this deletion was open to interpretation, but did not appear to change the intent of the legislation in the minds of the House committee. The deletion was interpreted by some as a move by the committee to win the support of several Congressmen who were concerned about additional aging programs in the heated debate over the Medicare issue.[38] Congress passed the bill in September 1962 and the President signed it into law (P.L. 87-838) on October 17, 1962, authorizing the new National Institute of Child Health and Human Development (NICHD).

Aging Research at NICHD

On January 30, 1963, the secretary of HEW approved the establishment of the National Institute of Child Health and Human Development with provisions that the Center for Aging Research and Center for Research in Child Health be transferred to the institute.

Aging advocates may have been somewhat optimistic because the proposed NICHD would include aging research within its program, incorporated into the broad scope of all stages of human life. It seemed a step forward: this was the first institute to focus on the life process rather than specific diseases. However, the institute's true focus on child health was set from the beginning and the director-designate of the new institute was a pediatrician, Dr. Robert Aldrich.

Aging research did not fare well in the new Institute for Child Health and Human Development. It was overshadowed not only by research in child health, but also by an emphasis on population (reproduction) research. Aging became one of five program areas in the institute designed to study the lifespan processes from fertility through adulthood: prenatal development and obstetrics, the health of children, mental retardation, population research, and aging. For the aging program, the existing NIH extramural and intramural programs in aging research were simply transferred to the new institute; thus, the extramural Center for Research in Aging established in 1956 to deflect the demands of the gerontologists, the intramural Gerontology

Research Branch in Baltimore, and intramural research from
the National Institute of Mental Health became the aging
program in the NICHD. The old Center for Research in Aging
became the Adult Development and Aging Branch of the new
NICHD.

Center for Research in Aging. The old center, long a
"paper organization," was somewhat of an embarrassment.
Wilbur J. Cohen, the assistant secretary of HEW, in
preparing a special Presidential Message on Aging, had
problems explaining the Center for Aging Research. In a
confidential memo to Surgeon General Luther S. Terry, he
wrote:

> This is, however, one area in which I feel we are weak,
> namely, the role of the Center for Aging Research in
> the NICHD. I would appreciate it therefore if you
> would prepare and send me a statement outlining in as
> much detail as possible a constructive program which
> the Center is undertaking or would undertake. We would
> then attempt to incorporate the essence of this in the
> Presidential message.[39]

Because the center had never implemented any programs, there
were none to describe; nor did the response to Cohen's
request describe any new program to be undertaken. Instead,
it summarized the center's vague and demonstrably ineffec-
tual responsibilities. To divert attention somewhat from
the center, however, an introductory paragraph about the
role of NIH was suggested for inclusion in the presidential
message. That role, typically, is to research categorical
diseases that afflict the elderly as well as young people:

> The National Institutes of Health have continued to
> increase their support of research on aging and the
> health problems of older persons. Significant ad-
> vances are being made against cancer, heart disease,
> arthritis, and other diseases which afflict the
> aged....
>
> The new Institute will assimilate the responsibilities
> and the functions of the Center for Aging Research
> which was created in 1956 to serve as a focus for
> aging research at the National Institutes of
> Health....[and] directly support gerontological
> research and training through the use of grants to
> universities, medical centers, and research institu-
> tions in this country and abroad. Research to be
> supported will encompass biological, medical, and
> behavioral aspects of the process of aging.[40]

<u>Gerontology Research Center.</u> From outward appearances, intramural aging research seemed to expand. The Gerontology Research Branch became the Gerontology Research Center and saw the official opening of a $7.5 million, four-story building located at and operated in cooperation with the Baltimore City Hospital in June 1968. In fact, the push for expansion of the Baltimore Center had been coming from outside NIH since 1940. The National Heart Institute appropriation for fiscal year 1962 had included $1 million for planning the proposed research facility built on the Baltimore City Hospital grounds. Building that center and maintaining its staff were a constant struggle. Maryland State Senator and chairman of the Maryland Commission on Aging, Margaret Collins Schweinhaut, other Baltimore officials, and allies such as Florence Stephenson Mahoney, a Georgetown resident who served on the council of NICHD, and her colleague Paul Glenn, a New York commodities broker who testified on behalf of aging programs at the Veterans Administration, kept Senator Lister Hill and Congressman Fogarty informed about the lack of support for the Baltimore Center. (Unfortunately, advocates of aging research lost their staunch ally, Fogarty, who died in January 1967.) As the following excerpts from a letter from Schweinhaut and the note from Glenn indicate, the provision of funds for

MEMO FROM   ⌐h 1-7
Paul F. Glenn

Nathan —

Florence believes that she has succeeded in unfreezing your 35 positions via the Budget Bureau. If you see no sign of this, call me right away.

2 12 - 7 12 2 -3251 Best —

Paul

a building and the authorization of additional positions
required persistent follow-up for implementation:

> The highest level possible of scientific staffing
> should be made. In order to "dicker" for such staff,
> always in short supply, it is important that authori-
> zation of them go forth currently, giving time for
> recruitment. The scientists presently working come
> from different parts of the world and it is hoped,
> once the new facility is available, it will be an
> irresistible [sic] "carrot" for renowned researchists.
> But there must be, as soon as possible, assurances that
> the money is there to pay them and that there is suffi-
> cient time for the scientists to adjust their own pres-
> ent careers in order to be available next fall....The
> Gerontological Research project was formerly under the
> Heart Institute of NIH but has been transferred to the
> Institute of Child Health and Human Development. The
> Congress last year authorized 35 additional positions
> for the Gerontological Research Center but none of
> these have been made available to the Center. Rather
> than a staff of 120, therefore, the Center now has
> only 82 and studies begun have had to be halted.[41]

Despite these efforts, however, the Baltimore Center did
not fulfill the hopes of gerontologists, as a member of
NICHD's Board of Scientific Counselors testified. Dr. F.
Marott Sinex, chairman of the Department of Biochemistry
and co-director of the Gerontology Center at Boston
University School of Medicine and president of the
Gerontological Society (1969-1970), stated in a 1971 Senate
Special Committee on Aging Report on Gerontological Research
that the Gerontological Research Center in Baltimore was
designed to be the largest center for aging research in the
world, but consistently operated at 50% or less of its
intended capacity. The original projected staff was 300,
but there were only 132 staff members in July 1968, and 120
in 1971. Sinex pointed out that the failure to staff the
center on an adequate basis and to conduct the kind of
gerontological research for which it was designed seemed to
reflect the relatively low priority accorded to research on
the aging process within the organizational structure of
NIH.[42]

NIMH Section. In addition to the Center for Aging Research
and the Baltimore Gerontological Research Center, NICHD
acquired the research initiatives from an Intramural Section
on Aging at the National Institute of Mental Health (NIMH).
Established in 1951, the NIMH section undertook a major
inter-institute, intramural research project in 1955 at the

Bethesda Clinical Center. The researchers, from physiology,
psychiatry, psychology, internal medicine, and other disciplines, were studying the interrelationships between psychological decline, changes in blood flow, and metabolism
in healthy aging men.[43] After the grant applications on
aging were directed to NICHD, the Section on Aging was ter-
minated. Nevertheless, NIMH continued to support extramural
research on aging. From 1966-1972 NIMH funded about $1.1
million in grants for basic behavioral research, $2.8 mil-
lion for clinical research, and $9.2 million for applied
research, including the demonstration of services for the
elderly.[44]

Dr. Carl Eisdorfer related the perspective of gerontologists
on the status of aging research within the Institute of
Child Health and Human Development in a statement before the
Special Senate Committee on Aging. He calculated that aging
research represented 8.79% of the total NICHD research budget ($3,233,799) and less than 0.03% of the NIH budget.[45]
This calculation was somewhat lower than NIH figures, but
as the following table shows, aging never accounted for more
than 11.9% of the NICHD budget through 1971.

National Institute of Child Health and Human Development
(dollar amounts in thousands)

Fiscal year	Total NICHD budget ($)	Total aging program budget ($)	Percentage of institute funds earmarked for research on aging
1964	30,461	3,036	10.0
1965	41,097	3,333	8.1
1966	53,434	5,068	9.5
1967	62,237	7,342	11.8
1968	66,830	7,973	11.9
1969	71,091	8,268	11.6
1970	76,506	8,100	10.6
1971	94,744	9,313	9.8

Source: Carl Eisdorfer, "Patterns of Federal Funding for
Research in Aging, The Gerontologist, 8 (Winter-Spring,
1967-68), p. 6.

The perspective had not improved by March 1971, when
Dr. Jerome Kaplan, president of the Gerontological Society,
testified at the joint hearings of the Senate special
Committee on Aging and the Subcommittee on Aging of the
Committee on Labor and Public Welfare. He began by saying
that the main characteristic of research and training in
the field of gerontology was that there was so little of
them. He quoted figures that illustrated a decline in
training funds at AoA and NICHD and that would not permit
new research in fiscal year 1972; some activities would
have to be cut back.[46]

Research Attempts at the Veterans Administration

Another federal agency, the Veterans Administration, having
perceived in the mid-1950's that the percentage of elderly
in its hospital population was fast increasing, from 5% in
1950 to 25% in 1960,[47] had begun researching diseases and
services related to aging. By 1964, the VA had organized
and initiated aging research centers, which soon met the
same fate as the centers at NIH.

The Satellite Laboratory Aging Program, conceived under the
VA Research Service in 1964, was initiated and guided by
Joe Meyer, Ph.D., Chief, Research in Basic Sciences, and
Harold Schnaper, M.D., Chief, Research in Internal Medicine. The purpose of the program was threefold: first, to
"focus more intensely on the mechanism of aging--an understanding of which will ultimately provide the means for
retarding or preventing aging-related disease and deterio-
ration...";[48] second, to induce "highly creative
scientists to give a significant amount of attention to the
problems of aging by making it possible for them to exploit
their ideas without the necessity of committing themselves
directly to the laboratory effort";[49] and third, to
"assure development of highly sophisticated research in
aging and bring first rate young scientists to the various
VA staffs." Within this unique program, university researchers were able "to undertake investigations of the
nature and causes of aging processes, which are related to
their particular areas of interest" at VA hospitals in
proximity to their affiliated universities,[50] a plan
feasible by virtue of the fact that the VA has one or more
hospitals near almost all major academic institutions.

The first satellite laboratory was installed in 1964 at the
VA Hospital in Bedford, Massachusetts, in conjunction with
the Boston University School of Medicine, coordinated by
Dr. Anthony P. Russel (VA), Dr. F. Marott Sinex (BU), and

Dr. R. L. Herrmann (BU). The VA's overall Accelerated Program of Research in Aging was undertaken "without any commitment of special funds. It was anticipated that the normal annual growth of research support would provide the necessary support from the FY-65 Budget."[51] Eight months after the first satellite program was in operation it became clear that, because of "directives for maximum economy in Government and the necessity to absorb the imminent pay raise," the Research in Aging Program would be left without any funds.[52]

In August 1964 a budget request was prepared for existing and proposed aging research in the VA which included three new satellite laboratories to start in fiscal year 1965. By the end of 1967, seven laboratories had been established.[53] Though the satellite program was never really viable, opinions were given that expressed the promise and significance of the satellite program. For example, a VA internal document states: "It is quite possible that within the next decade such research will generate some very practicle [sic] approaches to the aging problem and enable the VA to deal more appropriately with the shifting character of its patient population."[54] The program was known and encouraged on the Hill. In a letter to William Driver, the administrator of the Veterans Administration, Harrison Williams, chairman of the Senate Special Committee on Aging, notes that his committee is cognizant of the important impetus of the VA satellite laboratory concept in forwarding aging research and of the VA plans to expand this program as outlined in its report.[55] Driver's reply to Williams states:

> To date, only seven "satellite laboratories" for aging research have been brought into being. We believe that ultimately twenty of these should be developed. We estimate that approximately $250,000 is required to initiate one satellite laboratory program and that it would require a level of about $100,000 per year to maintain its high quality research.
>
> ...a number of important project types concerned with the biological processes of aging could be fruitfully developed and/or expanded in VA research facilities. This could be done by encouragement and mobilization of individual scientist projects into coordinated research in aging activities and/or expansion of the "satellite laboratory" programs, if funds are made available.[56]

By 1968, when Meyer left the VA, the program had already started to decline and by the end of the next year only

three satellite laboratories were in operation. Thus, the
VA effort to establish centers for aging research was one
more disillusionment for aging researchers in the 1960's.

By the end of the decade, the conviction was growing among
gerontologists that neither the NICHD nor any other federal
agency was meeting the demand for support for research on
aging. Although the issue had expanded sufficiently to be
on the public agenda, it failed to reach the formal agenda
of the government where it would be considered seriously.
The grievance deepened and the frustration of researchers
was coupled with distrust. They had in good faith put aside
their specific demand, generated at the 1961 White House
Conference, for a separate institute. They deferred to the
plans and promises of the president and NIH administration
to establish gerontology at NICHD as a viable research area
equal to the institute's other four program areas. Their
level of funding did not increase at NICHD, nor did their
visibility. Once again, they felt gerontology was being
hidden behind a facade. To make matters worse and the
future look gloomier, the Golden Years at NIH had ended.
If funds were to be had, gerontologists would have to
compete still harder. They could not survive without a
stronger base of public support. It became obvious that
strategies were needed to expand the issue even more to get
it on the formal agenda. A strategic step in the expansion
had been taken at the 1961 White House Conference when the
aging research issue was linked to preexisting issues related to the welfare of the elderly, but another step was
now needed to bring the research issue out of the welfare
shadow. The researchers who pushed for aging research at
the first White House Conference were a second-generation
cadre of professionals following in the footsteps of the
Club for Ageing Research who made the grievance known. This
second-generation cadre and their supporters would have to
involve still a larger audience in the expansion of the
issue. A second White House Conference in 1971 provided the
opportunity for that expansion and for a firm, united stand.
Meanwhile, legislative strategies were being mapped out by
individuals independent of the researchers.

                                NOTES

1. Roger Cobb, J.-K. Ross, and M. H. Ross, "Agenda
    Building as a Comparative Political Process," American
    Political Science Review, 70 (March 1976): 128.

2. Man and His Years (Raleigh, N.C.: Health Publications
    Institute, 1951), p. 261.

The members of the Section on Aging Research had made surveys and prepared reports prior to the conference in order to better formulate the research problems and to make their recommendations. The section's planning committee organized the subject into four topics: current research, including identification of active and neglected fields; identification of centers of research; research activities abroad; and sources of support for research. One survey conducted by the planning committee identified the few existing locations of research, chiefly within university departments. The planning committee had also prepared papers on research questions for study, touching on almost every area except economics: the problem of when aging begins; nutrition; cardiovascular problems; endocrine problems; skeletal, muscular, and joint problems; cancer; psychological, neuropsychiatric, and sociological problems.

3. Among the six members of the planning committee were Edmund V. Cowdry, research professor of anatomy at Washington University School of Medicine in St. Louis; Henry S. Simms, assistant professor of biochemistry at Columbia University College of Physicians and Surgeons; Clive M. McCay, professor of nutrition at Cornell; and a contributor to Cowdry's book, Oscar J. Kaplan, professor of psychology at San Diego State College. Nathan W. Shock from the Federal Security Agency and the Baltimore Center served as chairman for the secretariat of the section.

4. In his opening statement at the 1956 conference, Roswell B. Perkins, then assistant secretary of Health, Education, and Welfare and chairman of the Federal Council on Aging, defined the focus of the conference as federal and state responsibilities and interrelationships:

> This is not a national conference on aging. It is a working conference of primarily State and Federal officials. In recognizing this, I would like to articulate three thoughts which I am sure we all share: (a) A recognition that the solutions to the problems of older persons fundamentally lie with the individuals themselves and with their families; (b) a recognition that the great bulk of the contact with older persons outside of the families will be through our great structure of voluntary agencies, which are not and could not be represented adequately here today; and (c) a recognition that we are all talking only from present knowledge of the field of

aging, which is very limited and needs a great
deal of augmentation through practical research.
[Mobilizing Resources for Older People, Washington,
D.C.: GPO, 1957, p. 12.]

5. Stieglitz spoke to the Discussion Group on Physical and
Mental Health which recommended that:

2. Federal, State, and private agencies should provide
grant-in-aid funds for:

(a) Applied or operational research;
(b) The development and evaluation of demonstra-
tions of community health services for the
aged including the prevention of illness, the
detection of disease, the control of disability, and the rehabilitation of the individual;
and
(c) Basic research in gerontology. [Mobilizing
Resources, p. 60].

6. The White House Conference on Aging Act (P.L. 95-908),
85th Congress, H.R. 9822, September 2, 1982, Section
101 (6).

7. John Fogarty, quoted in The Nation and Its Older
People, DHEW, GPO: April 1961, p. 3.

8. Ibid.

9. Ibid.

10. The Nation and Its Older People, p. 5.

11. Michael March, memo to Roger Jones, January 21, 1958.

12. Reginald G. Conley, memo August 29, 1958.

13. Phillip S. Hughes, Assistant Director for Legislative
Reference, Bureau of the Budget, letter to the
president, August 30, 1958, p. 2.

14. Ibid.

15. The Nation and Its Older People, p. 5.

16. Ibid., p. 258.

17. Ibid., p. 240.

18. Ibid., pp. 240-241.

19. Ibid., p. 247.

20. Ibid., p. 249.

21. Michael March, memo to P. S. Hughes, September 5, 1958.

22. Stanley Mohler, interview, March 11, 1979.

23. Medicare was enacted in 1965 after about 18 years of effort to enact a program of national health insurance, and this was the compromise that resulted. Medicare was enacted at the same time as an extension of the Kerr-Mills Law (1960), and it proved to be seriously inadequate.

24. Carl Eisdorfer, "Patterns of Federal Funding for Research on Aging," The Gerontologist, 8 (Winter-Spring, 1967-68): 5.

25. Abraham Ribicoff, letter to Doris Johnson, March 24, 1961.

26. "Chronology of Events in Establishment of the National Institute of Child Health and Human Development," unpublished NICHD document, August 1, 1969, p. 24.

27. Ibid., p. 13.

28. John F. Kennedy, "Health Message to the Congress on February 9, 1961" in Ronald J. Wylie, Legislative History of the National Institute of Child Health and Human Development (unpublished NICHD document, August 1, 1969), p. 30.

29. Wylie, Legislative History, p. 23.

30. Ibid.

31. NIH director's memos to the Surgeon General, January 27, 1961 and January 31, 1961, in Wylie, Legislative History, pp. 25-26.

32. Wylie, Legislative History, from a discussion with Myer Feldman, p. 29.

33. "Establishment of a NICHD and NIGMS," March 1, 1961, in Wylie, Legislative History, p. 37.

34. Chief of Division of General Medical Sciences memo to the deputy director of NIH, June 14, 1961, in Wylie, Legislative History, p. 56.

35. Ibid.

36. Robert Havighurst, U.S. Congress, House, Subcommittee
    of the Committee on Interstate and Foreign Commerce,
    Child Health Institute, Hearings on H.R. 8398, 87th
    Congress, 2nd Session, February 13-14, 1962, p. 145.

37. Ewald W. Busse, February 13-14 Hearings.

38. During the Senate hearings, held on September 13, 1962,
    Mr. Boisfeuillet Jones' statement for the administra-
    tion included the following opinion concerning the
    deletion of the words "or aged persons":

>   (2) The provision authorizing the new Institute
>   of Child Health and Human Development as modified
>   to delete specific reference to health problems
>   and requirements of aged persons. Since this
>   modification was made by a floor amendment not
>   explained in the Committee report, the intent and
>   effect of this amendment are not entirely clear.
>   If its effect is only to make it permissive,
>   rather than mandatory, to include research on
>   aging within the scope of the new Institute's
>   program, the amendment would not be objectionable.
>   If, on the other hand, the amended provision should
>   be so construed as to preclude the assignment of
>   any significant aging research functions to this
>   new institute, we would strongly urge enactment of
>   the language of the Senate bill. Although some of
>   the key health problems of the aged will continue
>   to be studied through one or more of the categori-
>   cal institutes—such as, those in the field of
>   cancer and heart disease—there is also a need for
>   an integrated approach to study of the phenomena
>   and problems of aging in the continuum of human
>   development. An Institute of Child Health and
>   Human Development will, in our view, provide the
>   logical and appropriate setting for such study.

39. Wilbur J. Cohen memo to Luther S. Terry, January 4,
    1963.

40. Luther S. Terry memo to W. J. Cohen, January 14, 1963.

41. Margaret C. Schweinhaut letter to Lister Hill, February
    23, 1967.

42. F. Marott Sinex, "Bio-Medical Research on Aging," Re-
    search and Training in Gerontology, Special Committee

on Aging, U.S. Senate (Washington, D.C.: GPO, November 1971), p. 5.

43. James E. Birren, and V. J. Renner, "A Brief History of Mental Health and Aging," Issues in Mental Health: Research, vol. 1 (Washington, D.C.: GPO, National Institute of Mental Health, Pub. No. ADM 79-663, 1979), p. 11.

44. Research Task Force of the National Institute of Mental Health, Research in the Service of Mental Health, National Institute of Mental Health Pub. No. (ADM) 75-237 (Washington, D.C.: GPO, 1975), p. 41.

45. Carl Eisdorfer, Hearings on the Long-Range Program and Research Needs in Aging and Related Fields, Senate Special Committee on Aging, 90th Congress, 1st session, December 5-6, 1967, p. 202.

46. Jerome Kaplan, Evaluation of Administration on Aging and Conduct of White House Conference on Aging, Joint Hearings before the Special Committee on Aging and the Subcommittee on Aging of the Committee on Labor and Public Welfare, U.S. Senate (Washington, D.C.: GPO, March 25, 1971), p. 80-82.

47. Observation on Care of the Aging in Europe, House Committee Print No. 152, 87th Congress, 1st session, September 11, 1961 (Washington, D.C.: GPO, 1961), p. 1.

48. "VA Activities Affecting Older Veterans in 1969," Department of Medicine and Surgery, Veterans Administration, unpublished report, p. 8.

49. "VA Accelerated Program of Research in Aging," Veterans Administration, 151-B (August 6, 1964), unpublished report, p. 4.

50. "VA Activities," p. 8.

51. "VA Accelerated Program," p. 7.

52. Ibid.

53. Veterans Administration, unpublished report.

The three Satellite Laboratories in 1965 were the VA Hospital, Buffalo, New York, coordinated by Dr. Noel Rose (University of Buffalo Medical School); the VA Hospital, Baltimore, Maryland, coordinated by Dr.

Bernard Strehler (NIH Gerontology Institute); and VA
Hospital, Downey, Illinois, coordinated by Dr. Arthur
Veis (Northwestern University School of Medicine).

The laboratories in 1967 were: VA Hospital, Bedford,
Massachusetts, coordinated by Dr. Marott Sinex; VA
Hospital, Baltimore, Maryland, coordinated by Dr.
Bernard Strehler; VA Hospital, Downey, Illinois,
coordinated by Dr. Arthur Veis; VA Hospital, Buffalo,
New York, coordinated by Dr. Noel Rose; VA Hospital,
Sepulveda, California, coordinated by Dr. Linus
Pauling; and VA Hospital, Pittsburgh, Pennsylvania,
coordinated by Dr. Albert Lansing.

54. VA internal document, untitled, p. 3.

55. Harrison A. Williams, Jr., letter to William J.
     Driver, January 9, 1969.

56. W. J. Driver, letter to Harrison A. Williams, Jr., May
     23, 1969.

5
Entrance on the Formal Agenda

> Entrance represents movement from the public agenda to the formal agenda, where serious consideration of the issue by decision makers can take place.[1]

Although the 1961 White House Conference had given support for aging research visibility on the public agenda, entrance on the formal agenda as a bill seriously considered by Congress did not occur for another decade. Several "pseudo-agenda items" were introduced in the 1960's by legislators who had independent interests in an institute for aging research. Their efforts were premature, though they served a purpose in predisposing a few congressmen to later support a bill for an institute. The bill for an institute could not become viable until numerous senators and representatives agreed to support it, support generated by a confluence of uncoordinated efforts and circumstances. Access to key congressmen, the gatekeepers of Congress, was essential. Mrs. Florence Mahoney, gerontology researchers, and age-based interest groups lobbied in their independent fashions to get an institute for aging research on the formal agenda. The simultaneous efforts of these individuals and groups with different congressmen brought about the introduction of three bills on the formal agenda, all of which asked for a national focus for aging research. In the collection of bills, however, not only biomedical but also social and behavioral research were specified. This diversity of demands

was a reflection of the lack of unity among the various
pressure groups and individuals, and a signal that
compromise would be required to prevent even greater
frustration.

PSEUDO-AGENDA ITEMS

Pseudo-agenda items are bills introduced in Congress but not
given serious attention by the lawmakers; they have only
symbolic appeal for constituents. Such bills never or
seldom get hearings, are not considered by committees, and
thus never reach the floor of the House or the Senate. They
may be important, however, in creating an early awareness
that might later develop into interest.

The first such pseudo-agenda item regarding an institute
for aging research was the bill to amend the Public Health
Service Act to establish a National Institute of Geriatrics
(H.R. 3301) introduced by Edith Green (D-ORE) in 1959.
Hearings on the bill were never held and it was never
seriously considered by the Congress, though the administration was asked for an opinion.

In answer to a request from Representative Oren Harris,
chairman of the House Committee on Interstate and Foreign
Commerce, for comment on the bill, Robert A. Forsythe,
acting secretary of the Department of Health, Education,
and Welfare, responded that the National Institutes of
Health with its present institutes was conducting and
supporting a considerable amount of research in aging.[2]
Forsythe mentioned extramural grants for aging research
which totaled $4.1 million in 1959 and $5.5 million in 1960
for all the institutes. The administration's position
toward the bill was negative:

> In summary, we believe that the fostering and support
> of research in the health-related aspects of aging are
> now carried on and coordinated in an effective manner,
> with due regard to the fact that the various problems
> of aging are necessarily involved in the basic
> responsibilities of a number of the Institutes and
> other units of the Public Health Service, and that the
> establishment of a new statutory institute in the
> field of gerontology would not be a desirable step.[3]

The Bureau of the Budget, in preparing its response,
drafted several statements to the effect that the new
institute was "unnecessary and undesirable" or "would
result in undesirable inflexibility," and finally settled

on calling a National Institute of Geriatrics simply "undesirable."[4]

Though the Green bill never reached the formal agenda, there is some evidence that congressional members were becoming aware of the issue of aging research and a national institute of gerontology prior to the First White House Conference. Green introduced her bill in January 1959 and in May a Senate staff working paper included a suggestion to establish an institute for aging research. Under the leadership of Lister Hill, a new Subcommittee on the Problems of the Aging and Aged had been authorized for the Committee on Labor and Public Welfare on February 6, 1959. The staff document proposing an outline for the new subcommittee's work suggested the possibility of not only a national but also an international institute of gerontology for both biological and social sciences research.[5] The proposal failed to gain support and it never went forward for further consideration by the full committee. Several more pseudo-agenda items appeared. Representative William C. Cramer (R-FLA) introduced bills in 1963, 1967, and again in 1969 to establish an institute on gerontology at the Bay Pines Veterans Administration Center in his home state of Florida.[6]

In December of 1969, Representative William Springer of Illinois, an influential Republican noted for his conservatism and careful avoidance of legislative initiatives which would increase spending, introduced H.R. 15158 to establish a National Institute of Gerontology within the National Institutes of Health. The purpose of this institute would be to conduct and support "(1) research of treatments and cures for the diseases of the aged, and (2) training relating to such diseases and other special health problems and requirements of the aged...."[7] The bill focused on the biomedical aspects of aging research and did not refer to psychosocial areas of research.

Springer's request that this 1969 bill be drafted was a reaction to his personal experience with the problems of aging family members and ill health. He himself was near retirement and was bothered by the problems facing the increasingly large elderly population in the nation. Although he enjoyed good health and was only in his late 50's, he had vivid memories of caring for his aged father who was in and out of hospitals in Illinois for nine months before his death. In early December, Springer had received a birthday letter from one of his two older brothers. His brother had wished him a "Happy Birthday" and then went on at length about his own health problems and how difficult

it was to be getting old and miserable. Springer turned to
his secretary and asked her to have a staff member draft a
bill to create a national institute of gerontology.

Springer made these efforts solely on his own initiative.
Advocates of aging research had not lobbied Springer. Those
who were most informed and active in the cause of aging
research had no knowledge of the congressman's interest in
their cause.

Although Springer was the ranking minority member of the
House Committee on Interstate and Foreign Commerce whose
Subcommittee on Public Health and Environment handled
legislation related to NIH, his bill at the outset was
nothing more than a pseudo-agenda item; hearings were never
scheduled. Nevertheless, Springer's persistent interest in
an institute for aging research was valuable because it was
an early preparation for moving the issue from the public
agenda to the formal congressional agenda. Later, he would
continue to cosponsor bills which would become formal agenda
items.

PROMOTING THE REAL AGENDA ITEM

When the Springer bill was first introduced, even Florence
Mahoney, an advocate of aging research long eager to see
legislation to create an institute, was taken by surprise.
At the time his bill was introduced Mrs. Mahoney had already
been at work to get something going on the Senate side.
Though not an elected official nor an expert in aging
research, this individual had a significant influence on
the outcome of legislation to establish an institute for
aging research. She put dedication and energy, not money,
into her efforts and capitalized on the resources available
to her: contacts on the Hill and access to the gatekeepers
of Congress, a history of service to the Democratic party,
and personal charm.

As a young girl, Florence Mahoney had considered going to
medical school and took premedical courses in college;
although she never became a physician she did not lose her
keen interest in biomedical research and health. As early
as the 1930's she was instrumental in establishing mental
health programs in Georgia and had lobbied in that state
for birth control. By the time an institute for aging
research had been articulated as a specific demand, Mrs.
Mahoney had had considerable success and experience in the
politics of health. She was well known on Capitol Hill, at
the National Institutes of Health, and in the scientific

community for the efforts she and her colleague, Mary
Lasker, had made on behalf of medical research.

Florence Mahoney and Mary Lasker met shortly after World
War II because their husbands, Daniel Mahoney, a publisher
in the Cox newspaper chain, and Albert D. Lasker, a wealthy
advertising executive, were friends.[8] The Laskers and
the Mahoneys had been active in the Democratic party and
both knew important legislators and key government
officials. The two women soon learned that they shared a
strong interest in health issues--birth control, mental
health, and biomedical research. They were both convinced
that the momentum biomedical research had gained from the
federal financing during World War II should not be lost.

Mrs. Lasker and Mrs. Mahoney first joined efforts in pursuit
of their mutual goals by supporting Senator Claude Pepper
of Florida in his bid for reelection in 1944 because they
were aware that he planned to hold hearings on the state of
the nation's health.[9] The Lasker-Mahoney strategy was
comprehensive and focused. Mr. Lasker would support the
Pepper campaign with dollars and Mr. Mahoney would provide
editorial endorsement of his candidacy in the Miami Daily
News. Mrs. Lasker and Mrs. Mahoney asked Senator Pepper to
devote a portion of the Senate hearings to the future of
biomedical research, and he agreed to cooperate.

The early success was the beginning of a long friendship
and commitment to the cause of federal support for medical
research. During the 1950's and 1960's, Mrs. Lasker and
Mrs. Mahoney were seen as a team of dedicated, intelligent,
energetic women with an elite group of associates who
served as catalysts behind the scenes in Washington to
foster and direct the course of biomedical research in this
country.[10] The Laskers became active in the American
Cancer Society, and through their Lasker Foundation for
Medical Research, rewarded scientists and public officials
who advanced research. They also made substantial contributions to the campaigns of candidates whom they thought would
have an interest in medical research. They employed skilled
professional lobbyists and, with the able assistance of
Mrs. Mahoney, used the mass media to inform the public
about their cause. The "Lasker Lobby," as the effort
became known, formed an unbeatable coalition with "Mr.
Health," Senator Lister Hill, and his colleague in the
House, Congressman John Fogarty, to make medical research
policy and history during two decades of the Golden Era.

In the late 1960's, Mrs. Lasker began to organize an
all-out crusade against cancer, but this time Florence

Mahoney would not be available to help.[11]   Her interest
in a national institute for aging research required her
full attention.   During her work with Mary Lasker over the
years, Florence Mahoney had served as a lay member on
several national health advisory groups.   She was a member
of the National Mental Health Council for NIH from 1951 to
1955 and the National Advisory Council for Arthritis and
Metabolic Diseases from 1959 to 1963.   NIH officials recall
Mrs. Mahoney's outspoken support for aging research from
the time she served on the Arthritis Council.[12]   In the
late 1950's she had prepared witnesses in her Georgetown
home to testify on behalf of aging research programs in the
Veterans   Administration.[13]   She   and   her   friend   Paul
Glenn[14] had had some success in getting support for the
Baltimore Gerontological Research Center, but she felt
increasingly thwarted in her efforts to foster the cause of
aging research as she served on the National Advisory
Council for Child Health and Human Development from its
founding in 1963 to 1967.   She was convinced that aging
research was not going to get the support it should have
within the framework of NICHD.

Though determined to campaign for research causes, she
decided not to use the press as a strategy for aging
research.   The subject was difficult to treat in newspaper
articles, and she felt there was not much her friends from
the press could do with the topic.   There was no institute
at NIH that one could point to as a place where action
could be taken.   The House of Representatives did not have
a committee on aging to which one could appeal.   She
believed the public would not be as interested in aging as
it was in cancer and heart disease.   She could not interest
her friend Mary Lasker in the possibilities of research on
aging.   Like the early opponents to aging research at NIH,
Mrs. Lasker and many others thought that solving the
problems related to heart disease and cancer would solve
the problems of aging.

Even though Florence could not convince her friends that
aging research was important, she knew how to work behind
the scenes with Congress to get support for research.   She
knew that Senator Tom Eagleton (D-MO) had expressed an
interest in aging research but felt that as a matter of
courtesy she should first go to the Chairman of the Senate
Committee on Labor and Public Welfare, Senator Ralph
Yarborough from Texas.   She asked Yarborough to introduce a
bill to create an institute on aging.   The senator was
polite but did nothing.   She kept after him but without
results.   Finally, she talked to Eagleton, whom she knew
socially, and he said he would introduce a bill if she
could get a substantial number of influential cosponsors.

Florence Mahoney set about to get those cosponsors on her own. She recruited medical students and their young friends to help her gain additional support. One, Charles A. Welch, had come to Washington in the spring of 1970 to represent a group of medical students and faculty from Boston who were concerned about the shootings at Kent State and the bombing of Cambodia. One of his professors, Dr. F. Marott Sinex, sent him to Florence Mahoney for guidance on how to form a lobby of medical professionals against the war in Vietnam.

Her advice was to concentrate on medical issues instead. She convinced him that the people on the Hill were sick of hearing about the war and would welcome an opportunity to focus on another issue. What was needed was a progressive lobbying force in medicine. Florence helped Welch and others lobby for grants for medical students and for national health insurance, coaching them on how to testify and approach individual senators and representatives to win support. They in turn spent the summer of 1970 helping her lobby for an institute.

Florence Mahoney personally visited many of the key senators, representatives, and their staffs and succeeded in getting thirty-eight congressmen to say they would be willing to either cosponsor or vote for a bill to create a National Institute of Aging. To impress Eagleton with the amount of support the bill could get, she coached her young friends in ways to persuade people on the Hill that aging, as a science and as a social issue, was important enough to deserve institute status at NIH. At times she even took the young, unsure students to the doors of senator's offices and literally pushed them in. Her efforts succeeded. Senators Saxbe, Javits, and Brook were receptive. Although the students were from Boston, Kennedy's staff would not take time to listen to their ideas.[15]

As part of her lobbying activities, Florence Mahoney, a gracious hostess, entertains in her Georgetown home. Those whom she would persuade are charmed and delighted by her dinner parties. She was entertaining dinner guests one evening when she received a telephone call from an angry Yarborough who had learned that she approached Eagleton and others about the bill for an aging institute. He wanted an explanation of her actions. She assured the senator that she was only trying to assist him, that knowing how busy he was as chairman she felt it would make things easier for him if she got another committee member to take on some of the work. Yarborough was not placated by her response, but fortunately for Mrs. Mahoney he failed to regain his senate seat in 1970. Senator Harrison Williams replaced Yarborough on the Senate Committee on Labor and Public Welfare, and

Mrs. Mahoney lost no time in telling Williams that Eagleton
should shepherd the bill to create an institute. Williams
agreed. In 1971 Eagleton became chairman of the Subcommittee on Aging of the Committee on Labor and Public Welfare.

On February 19, 1971, Senator Eagleton, along with fourteen
influential cosponsors[16] introduced S. 887, which proposed a National Institute of Gerontology. When Eagleton
introduced the bill in the Senate, he described the proposed
institute as "filling the gap" in research efforts and
cited statistics on the current and projected size of the
elderly population. He pointed out that during the last
year only about seven-tenths of 1% of the total NIH research
budget went for research to alleviate the problems of
elderly citizens. Eagleton called such a meager allocation
not only inequitable but also short-sighted because
two-thirds of total expenditures for health care can be
attributed to treating elderly persons at a time when,
according to recognized medical authorities, medical
knowledge regarding aging and degenerative diseases has
reached a point where major breakthroughs could be made.
Eagleton spoke about the new institute's great potential
for improving the "quality of life of the aged" and for
leading to "an extension of the healthy middle years of
life" by improving knowledge of the aging process.[17]

The Senate bill would create an institute to conduct and
support not only biomedical research and training but also
social and behavioral research relating to the aging
process. This broadening of the mandate was not a result
of Florence Mahoney's efforts. She felt strongly that the
new institute at NIH should be devoted solely to biomedical
research and that to include psychosocial and behavioral
research would spread resources too thin and would delay
biomedical breakthroughs. She saw the Administration on
Aging as the appropriate agency for the support of social
science research, not NIH. Many biomedical scientists and
other advocates of aging research agreed with her about the
more narrow focus for an institute on aging; nevertheless,
she said nothing about the wording in the bill because she
felt that internal conflicts would threaten passage of the
bill.

A PLAN FOR AGING RESEARCH

Three months after Eagleton introduced his bill, Senator
Harrison Williams (D-NJ), chairman of the Senate Labor and
Public Welfare Committee and chairman of the Senate Special
Committee on Aging until 1971, introduced "The Research on

Aging Act, a bill to promote the advancement of research in aging through a comprehensive and intensive program for the systematic study of the aging process in human beings" (S. 1925). The bill called for the establishment of an Aging Research Commission which would be responsible for developing a long-range program, to be known as the gerontological research plan, designed to promote intensive, coordinated research into biological, medical, psychological, social, and economic aspects of aging.

As he introduced the bill, Williams proudly pointed out that his bill had the "strong support of the Gerontological Society, a longstanding leader in the field of geriatric research."[18] The senator did not add that the support from the Gerontological Society came only after the original form of the bill, The Preliminary Gerontological Research Act (S. 3784) introduced in July 1968, designed to promote biological research in aging, had been substantially revised to require that the plan of the proposed commission include medical, psychological, social, and economic aspects of aging. Williams and his staff had been aided in the drafting of the original bill by a well-known and somewhat controversial biomedical researcher, Dr. Bernard Strehler, from the University of Southern California, who had been working on this idea for some time. Strehler's idea called for a quinquennial research plan to promote intensive, coordinated research on the biological origins of aging. Strehler took a copy of the 1968 bill to the annual Gerontological Society meeting held in Denver, Colorado, and asked his colleagues to give the bill the formal endorsement of the society. Society officials firmly resisted this suggestion on the basis that the society was a multidisciplinary group and that all aspects of the aging process must be studied if progress were to be made. Strehler did not mince words in his criticism of the society and its officials for not supporting his bill.

The president of the society, Dr. Bernice Neugarten, a prominent psychologist in the field of aging at the University of Chicago, and members of the society's Public Policy Committee said that the bill could be endorsed if it were revised to include the social sciences. Neugarten and two of the committee members, Dr. Marott Sinex and Dr. Robert Binstock, revised Strehler's bill and then paid a visit to Bill Oriol, staff director of the Senate Special Committee on Aging, on January 15, 1969, to explain their concern that the bill was limited to a plan for biomedical research and did not include the social sciences. Neugarten was adamant about the need for social science research and assured Oriol that the Gerontological Society would never

support the bill in its present form, that members of the
society would write letters opposing it and publicly testify
against it. Oriol listened carefully as Neugarten and her
colleagues explained their reasons for wanting modifica-
tions. He then asked the society to submit its own version
of the bill for consideration by the committee. They
submitted the version they had already prepared. Sinex, a
past president of the Gerontological Society, tried then
and later to act as mediator between the biologists and
social scientists because he was "afraid war would break
out and blow the whole thing up."[19]

Although the Senate Special Committee on Aging does not
have authority to report bills to the floor, it has had,
throughout its history, an influence on legislation as an
originator of proposed legislation, as a watchdog over
legislative developments related to the aged, and as an
internal lobby for legislation.[20] In the case of
legislation to create an institute on aging, the committee
served as a legislative catalyst in all three ways.

NOTES

1.   Roger Cobb, J.-K. Ross, and M. H. Ross, "Agenda Build-
     ing as a Comparative Political Process, The American
     Political Science Review, 70 (March 1976): 129.

2.   Robert A. Forsythe letter to Oren Harris, May 5, 1960,
     p. 1:

          The Center for Aging Research at the National
          Institutes of Health operates as liaison for the
          National Institutes of Health in the field of
          aging. This Center helps to coordinate the
          research conducted by the Institutes and similar
          research conducted by other agencies and
          organizations. The Gerontology Branch of the
          National Heart Institute, a component of this
          Institute since the Institute's establishment in
          1948, conducts basic and clinical research on
          aging. The Section on Aging in the National
          Institute of Mental Health has studied psychologi-
          cal aspects of aging for more than five years.

3.   Ibid., p. 3.

4.   Phillip S. Hughes letter to O. Harris, May 9, 1960.

5. "Outline on the Subcommittee's Work," internal staff document of the Subcommittee on Problems of the Aged and Aging, May 1959:

> There is some research taking place in the field of aging federally, but it is incidental to many other things, and we probably will make real progress only when a designated specialty develops. We need to explore quickly the need for a national institute of gerontology as a national and international research center in the biological and social aspects of aging. (Perhaps this ought to be an international institute of gerontology.)

6. House Joint Resolution 286, 90th Congress, 1st Session, February 9, 1967.

7. H.R. 15158, 91st Congress, 1st Session, December 9, 1969, pp. 1-2.

8. Florence Mahoney, telephone conversation, May 5, 1980.

9. Ibid.

10. See Stephen P. Strickland, Politics, Science and Dread Disease (Cambridge: Harvard University Press, 1976), for a vivid description of the joint efforts of Mrs. Lasker and Mrs. Mahoney in the early years of the "Lasker Lobby" initiatives.

11. See Richard A. Rettig, Cancer Crusade: The Story of the National Cancer Act of 1971 (N.J.: Princeton University Press, 1977), for detailed information on the lobbying efforts for cancer research.

12. John F. Sherman, interview, June 14, 1978.

13. Interviews with Joe Meyer, Stanley Mohler, F. Marott Sinex, and Florence Mahoney.

14. Paul Glenn, with encouragement from Mrs. Mahoney, later created the Glenn Foundation for Medical Research, a foundation devoted primarily to research on aging.

15. Mahoney, May 5, 1980.

16. The fourteen original cosponsors were: Bayh, Bible, Dole, Harris, Hart, Humphrey, Inouye, Jackson, McGovern,

88   Building the Agenda

Montoya, Nelson, Pell, Spong, and Tunney. By September
1972 when the bill was reported out of committee with
amendments, it had twenty-seven cosponsors.

17. Thomas Eagleton, Congressional Record-Senate, 92nd
Congress, 1st Session, February 19, 1971, p. 3290.

18. Harrison Williams, Congressional Record-Senate, 92nd
Congress, 1st Session, May 21, 1971, p. 16386.

19. F. Marott Sinex, interview, July 25, 1968.

20. See Dale Vinyard, "The Senate Special Committee on the
Aging," The Gerontologist (Autumn 1972), esp. pp.
298-303, for an analysis of the roles and functions of
the Senate Special Committee on the Aging as a
mechanism created by political systems as a generalized
response to older persons.

II
Legislation for an Institute

6
Getting the Senate Bill Passed

With the issue's entrance on the formal congressional agenda, the agenda-building process yields to the legislative
process. New actors and events influence the outcome of the
demand for a national institute for aging research. Though
Florence Mahoney played the lead role in getting the attention of the gatekeepers of Congress, she was not alone in
promoting the idea of an institute. The Gerontological
Society would supply key witnesses at hearings and recruit
other interest groups in the lobbying efforts. The senators
and representatives who were gatekeepers at the time of the
issue's entrance on the formal agenda would become active
sponsors of the bill. Congressional committees and subcom-
mittees and their chairpersons and staffs were crucial to
the bill's career, as were congressional majority and
minority leaders and witnesses at hearings. The timing of
events was critical--the scheduling of hearings and debates
and the placement of the bill for vote on Senate and House
calendars. Even external events, such as political conven-
tions and elections, influenced the outcome of the bill.
The critical event came in 1971 between hearings on the
Senate bills. A second White House Conference on Aging
expanded the aging issue and gained greater public interest
and pressure and attracted the attention of government
policy makers.

91

On the whole, however, more and stronger forces seemed to be working against the establishment of an institute than for it. President Nixon was opposed to the institute. The administration at DHEW and NIH were opposed to it, arguing against a proliferation of institutes and insisting that the current structure at NICHD provided adequate support for the amount of research leads in aging. Even Congress was wary of new institutes at a time when the "disease of the month club" was a slogan and six other institutes had been proposed. The NIH era of Golden Years had ended and the Republican administration was trying to cut the federal budget and reduce personnel. The biomedical aging research issue did not have the backing of a mass media campaign, a powerful lobby, nor the scientific community at large. The advocates of an institute did not constitute an organized coalition; to the contrary, they had serious divergences of interest in the purpose of an institute. Clearly, the demand for an institute on aging did not enter the formal agenda with the typical supportive forces that pressure the passage of a bill into law.

EARLY HEARINGS ON THE SENATE BILL

Ten days after Senator Williams had introduced his bill to establish an Aging Research Commission, the Senate Subcommittee on Aging held the first of three day-long hearings (June 1, 2, and 14) on Eagleton's bill and Williams' bill.

In an effort to accommodate Senator Ted Kennedy (D-MA), the new chairman of the Health Subcommittee, Senator Eagleton, as the new chairman of the Subcommittee on Aging, had agreed to include in the hearings Kennedy's bill (S. 1163) on nutrition for the elderly. The Kennedy bill provided for grants to the states for low-cost meal programs and for nutrition training and education programs for the elderly. Although combining these three bills into one hearing resulted in testimonies jumping back and forth between nutrition and research, Eagleton apparently felt that the effort to cooperate with his Democratic colleague was worthwhile.

The first day of the hearing was devoted exclusively to the subject of aging research and the best organizational means to achieve national objectives for such research. Statements were presented by the president of the National Council of Senior Citizens, by a representative of the American Association of Retired Persons and the National Retired Teachers Association, and by four gerontological researchers. Strehler sent a written statement.

Position of the Sponsors

In his introductory remarks, Senator Eagleton pointed out the different structural mechanisms in his bill and Senator Williams' bill, but emphasized that "Both of these bills have the same goal: To coordinate and greatly increase research in aging. The governmental mechanisms proposed by each to achieve this goal vary somewhat, but I am confident we can work together to reconcile such differences as may exist in the two bills."[1]

In addition, he made two points about funding. First, he commented on the "remarkable" budgetary cutbacks recommended by the administration and emphasized that the research funds under Title IV of the Older Americans Act had been increased to $2.8 million--the same figure as the previous year--only after joint hearings of his subcommittee and the Special Committee on Aging demonstrated the drastic effects of the proposed reductions. Second, Eagleton pointed out that the bill under consideration in the hearings would not, of itself, provide increased appropriations for aging research.

Senator Williams, after mentioning in his opening statement the timeliness of these hearings in light of the fact that the second White House Conference on Aging was only a few months away, made a point that was restated in nearly all of the public statements in the Senate proceedings on the new institute--aging research should have more funding. Williams agreed with Eagleton that "Regardless of the approach--whether it is a National Institute of Gerontology, an Aging Research Commission, or something else--I am hopeful that the subcommittee will act promptly and favorably in establishing a single governmental unit for promoting and coordinating aging research."[2]

Senator Frank Church (D-ID), then chairman of the Senate's Special Committee on Aging, testified very strongly on behalf of Eagleton's bill, but said nothing about the Williams bill.

Citizens Groups: Strength in Numbers

The National Council of Senior Citizens sent its president and seasoned lobbyist, Nelson Cruikshank, who immediately pointed out that he was representing more than three million members of the affiliated organizations of the National Council. After commending the committee for its interest in the problems of the aged, he noted that it is "heartening

to older Americans everywhere to note that a committee--and
if I may so say, a subcommittee headed by such a young
Senator--is taking an interest in the problems, the serious
problems that confront older Americans today."[3] Cruikshank's testimony soon ranged over the economic landscape
--from the over one billion dollars a year savings of a
breakthrough in the delay of senile dementia to the
"woefully inadequate" budget figures of the administration
which, in the light of inflation, represented about a 20%
cutback in funds available for aging research.[4]

Cruikshank was very direct about the National Council's
support for including social science research in the
proposed institute. He said the emphasis should be on "the
whole man" and cited his organization's success in lifting
the economic status of elderly people, which, in turn,
brought them out of what had appeared to be the decay of
senility. Cruikshank expressed emphatic support for
Eagleton's bill, termed Williams' bill "another useful
approach," and urged the subcommittee to merge the features
of the two bills and "thus ease the process of enactment."

Concluding his formal statement on a light note, Cruikshank
recounted a recent discussion with a woman celebrating her
85th birthday. When he commented how wonderful it was that
medical science had given her an additional 20 years of
life she replied with a snort, "It would be great if medical
science would add 20 years to the age between 39 and 40."[5]

Cyril Brickfield of the American Association of Retired
Persons and the National Retired Teachers Association
caught everyone's attention with the statement that he
represented 2,700,000 older Americans. One witness
observed that after Brickfield let them know the size of
his constituency, the "Senators who had been almost asleep
during previous testimony now sat up like wire-haired
terriers."[6] Brickfield's major concern was that the
budget for aging research for the years 1964 through 1972
at the National Institute of Child Health and Human
Development showed support for aging research going "down,
down, down, all the time."[7]

The millions represented by Brickfield and Cruikshank
constituted the kind of popular support for aging research
that was crucial. These groups had voiced their support
for an Aging Institute at the first White House Conference,
but now the members of Congress became aware of the mass
public support that aging research could generate. The
scientists were learning that to hold the attention of

Congress they needed the help of these lay groups who were gaining visibility and who spoke a language Congress understands. In fact, officials of the Gerontological Society had approached Brickfield and Cruikshank and supplied them with information for their statements. For Congress, the technical language of the biomedical researchers about the need for breakthroughs related to DNA and cell biology to understand the aging process was less compelling.

Position of Individual Scientists

Dr. Marott Sinex seemed to recognize this communication gap between the researchers and the legislators and tried to address it in his testimony when he assured the subcommittee that there was enough basic knowledge to lead to further meaningful discovery: "Aging is not a great scientific mystery. The fact that people think that it is [sic] a cultural thing. It is a matter of cultural attitude, not a reason matter. It is true that we do not know all we should know about aging. While we lack some basic information, there is also a need to evaluate what we know and apply what we have already learned."[8] Sinex, experienced advisor in gerontology to the extramural program of NIH and on the Intramural council of Advisors of NICHD, pointed out that the cost of not aggressively pursuing aging research is great. Sinex focused on the economic aspects of a decrease in productivity during older age and the financial impacts on the federal budget.

Sinex touched on several points that would resurface time and again in the three years of hearings. Witnesses would emphasize that the president's budgetary cutback of approximately $1.3 million in 1971 for research on aging meant that there would be no competitive renewals and no innovative grants funded: "...expansion of this field of research is dead. Those who are unlucky enough to have their grants come up for renewal in the year of the White House Conference on Aging have had it."[9] Sinex said that the intramural Gerontology Research Center in Baltimore had never been staffed anywhere near a sufficient level to utilize the facility as it was originally intended. In his opinion, "the necessity for a certain amount of investigation, which might not win the NIH another Nobel Prize next year, has placed the Center in Baltimore in a rather defensive position. It is half funded and half occupied, but still envied and with some perplexing staffing problems."[10] Asked why not simply create a center out of the aging program within the existing NICHD structure,

Sinex responded that while a center might well be a
short-term interim step toward creating an institute,
centers traditionally do not provide a full range of
functions, for example, they do not ordinarily include
intramural components.

Eagleton was particularly interested in what the other
institutes had been doing in the aging field and whether
establishing a new institute might induce them to phase out
present aging research activities. Sinex discounted the
possibility and replied that even though NICHD had the chief
responsibility for aging research, the largest existing
program was in the National Institute of Mental Health
where about 1.5% of the budget was related to the aging
process.

After estimating a budget of about $20 million for the
beginning operations of the proposed institute, Sinex
speculated that NICHD "would be willing to see the aging
operation go if it went in a way that would not curtail--and
might actually help their basic program areas, which they
see as pediatrics, obstetrics, and mental retardation.
Population research has been thrust upon them."[11]

Attention dramatically turned to the lack of opportunities
for talented, interested scientists to actually do research
consistent with their training in the aging field. Sinex
had brought along a colleague, Dr. William Hettinger,
formerly an advanced training grantee of NICHD. Hettinger
told about his own training, a story that was picked up and
used in all later legislative proceedings about the National
Institute on Aging. Hettinger was a physical chemist and,
about ten years earlier, as a result of some research he
was doing, had become intrigued by the aging problem from a
number of standpoints. He left a position in private
industry in which he had directed 100-150 researchers for
ten years to accept a three-year training fellowship in
what he considered a very challenging and exciting research
area that responded to great social and human need. In
anticipating the completion of the program, he made a major
effort to find a way of putting his training to work in
government or industry, but had no success. He finally
concluded that there was no place or way to put the training
to work even though the government had invested over $60,000
in that training. Hettinger returned to industry as an
industrial chemist.[12]

Likewise, Dr. Carl Eisdorfer, professor of psychiatry and
director of the Center for Study of Aging in Human Development, Duke University, said that his strong support for
Eagleton's bill derived from the experience that the current

structure for aging research was inadequate, even though he
had previously supported the idea of a branch at NICHD:
"...a few years ago I might not have given my wholehearted
support to such a bill, but times have proved me wrong.
Through no fault of those persons responsible for the aging
program in the NIH, the structure of that organization has
failed to be adequate to its mission."[13] Eisdorfer hit
on the hard facts of the budget; not only would increased
funding for NICHD go primarily to the Population Control
Center, but, in addition, funds would be cut from the aging
program in order to bring population and child health
programs up to the desired levels. Approximately $3
million for the Population Center would have to be picked
up by cutting the existing programs within the institute.
The budget of the Adult Development and Aging Branch in
NICHD had already dropped from 10% to about 9% or below in
the previous year and would have to give up even more
funds. Eisdorfer emphasized that aging research was not
even holding the line at NIH and that the situation for
training was equally bad if not worse. He said that he did
not know of one NICHD fellow trained for aging research who
had gotten a job in aging--their stories all resembled
Hettinger's. Eisdorfer pointed out that even though there
are no jobs, a lot of people want to study in the field.
The Duke program alone received approximately fifty applications a year for its program.

The last witness on this day of hearings was a researcher
who would serve as the standard bearer for biomedical
researchers throughout subsequent hearings. Dr. Denham
Harman, chairman of the American Aging Association (known
as AGE), explained that his association had been formed
only a few months earlier, chiefly by members of the
biological sciences section of the Gerontological Society
who had become increasingly concerned about the need for
more biological research on aging. The group was established as a lay-scientific organization to promote
biomedical aging research and to inform the public of
preventive medicine and the progress of aging research. As
spokesman for the group, Harman was highly supportive of
the bill to establish an institute for aging research,
insisting that now was the time to increase emphasis on
biomedical aging research because the practical limit of
man's ability to increase life expectancy through conven-
tional disease-oriented research was about to be reached.
He noted that life expectancy had not increased since 1955,
and said, "We need to know what determines the rate of
aging....To understand the nature of the so-called biological clock and how to control its rate should be a major
focus of biomedical aging research. If we can slow up the
clock we can get more years of healthy life."[14]

The Administration's Position

The administration's witnesses, originally scheduled to appear during the June 1 and 2 hearings, requested that their appearance be postponed to allow additional time to formulate the administration's position on the legislation, thus requiring an extra day of hearings on June 14, 1971. Stephen Kurzman, the assistant secretary for legislation in DHEW, presented a prepared statement. He was accompanied by John Martin, commissioner, Administration on Aging, and Dr. Robert Q. Marston, director, National Institutes of Health, who did not present statements but did respond to questions from the chairman.

Kurzman recognized the increasing public and congressional interest in the problems of aging, both physiological and social; expressed the administration's concern for reform of income maintenance; and predicted that the amendments to the Social Security Act (H.R. 1) "will have the most significant impact on the well-being of the elderly of any single piece of legislation in decades."[15]   Two arguments articulated by Kurzman would emerge on behalf of the administration in every set of hearings on the institute proposals.

The first argument was that the aging field is not really ready for support:

> ...experience in the management of biomedical research programs makes it very evident that no mere organization change—of and by itself—can cause a research effort to flourish. The irreducible need is for a substantial body of interested and competent research investigators, plus enough research leads, or promising ideas within the field to challenge the researchers to productive endeavors. Only if these preconditions are met can one say that a particular research area is ripe for the injection of major new resources.[16]

That argument was later refuted by the Senate Committee on Labor and Public Welfare in its report as a "self-fulfilling prophecy" because researchers are influenced by the priorities funded by NIH. The report recognized that the results of researchers internationally "can reasonably be expected to point the way to advances."[17]

The second argument was that there are too many institutes proliferating:

During each session of recent Congresses there have been enough proponents of this theory to cause the introduction of bills to establish up to half a dozen or more institutes within the National Institutes of Health. In the current session of Congress, for example, there are proposals for five new institutes. In addition to the one to be created by this bill, new institutes are proposed for marine medicine, for digestive disease, for kidney disease, and for sickle cell anemia.[18]

Kurzman further argued that the Congress would be reversing its own earlier position when it created the National Institute of Child Health and Human Development on the basis that one institute should study the entire lifespan processes because the physiological and psychological events of childhood may have profound effects on health, disease, and longevity in adulthood.

Refuting these arguments in its report, the committee concluded that overlapping responsibilities cannot always be avoided in scientific research and "indeed, they may sometimes be desirable." The committee gave the director of NIH considerable flexibility in assigning responsibility for research and training to the new institute or to another institute when both institutes have functions relating to the same subject matter. However, the committee cautioned that it was "not intended that this authority be used as a device to bypass the National Institute on Aging...."[19] Because the Senate bill mandated behavioral as well as biomedical research, the committee required that social scientists, along with biomedical scientists and public representatives, be on the Advisory Council of the institute.

Finally, the administration claimed that NIH was presently supporting a "respectable" aging research effort and had recently directed Arthur Flemming, chairman of the 1971 White House Conference on Aging, to appoint a Task Force to examine the future status and role of the Administration on Aging and report its findings to the conference. Kurzman reported that Flemming was anticipating that the Task Force would also look at the role and status of the president's Council on Aging and that until the recommendations of both the Task Force and the White House Conference on Aging are available, "we do not favor action on S. 1925."[20]

Apparently to put into question the administration's claim of a "respectable" level of support for aging research,

Eagleton entered on the record a letter dated April 8,
1971, from Dr. Gerald LaVeck, director of NICHD, addressed
to Dr. Denham Harman, which confirmed a $1.4 million
reduction in aging research funds for fiscal year 1972 as
compared to funds spent in fiscal year 1971 for this
program. This will mean, wrote LaVeck, "for example, that
no new aging research grant awards can be made in fiscal
year 1972."[21]

Before adjourning the hearings, Eagleton addressed a number
of pointed questions to Dr. Robert Marston. Marston took a
position which would become common to NIH witnesses, namely,
that most of the NIH budget, one way or another, relates to
the problems of older people, that the problems of genetics,
of endocrinology, and of bones, for example, are all problems of aging. Marston urged that the question of organization be clearly separated from the question of budget. He
mentioned that pulmonary diseases, population research, and
sickle cell anemia programs had had substantial increases
of funds without the creation of new institutes. The NIH
director made it clear that his agency's budget was tight
and that cuts for aging research should not be interpreted
as a lack of interest or commitment, but simply as a matter
of balancing the various programs at a time when funds and
positions were scarce.

With Marston's assurance that the administration has always
wanted to be "responsive to the view of Congress" ringing
in his ears, Eagleton became very direct: "How does
Congress club you over the head into doing that [putting
more emphasis on aging]...without mandating a change in the
organizational structure?"[22]

Marston responded with the suggestions that funds be
increased, that research opportunities be considered, and
that the amount of the funding increase is justified and
does not interfere "with the very good job that is being
done, in many of the disease areas which are directly
related to the aging problem."[23]

Senator Eagleton persisted, "So what alternative do you
leave us?..." Marston replied that the historical precedent
of pairing increased funding with establishing a new
institute, as was done with the National Eye Institute and
the Environment Health Science Institute, is not necessarily
advisable:

     I can tell you that in both of these instances, the
     creation of a new institute at NIH with the buildup of
     the whole logistical and support background, has carried

a cost. I am not saying that in either of these in-
stances a mistake was made, but I am saying that it is
not as it was 5 or 10 years ago when creation of a new
institute was followed by markedly increased resources
because it had been named an institute.[24]

Eagleton became less hostile in asking for specific ideas
on means to increase aging research:

> I think that you and the administration showed remark-
> able cooperation in the recent give and take...in the
> war on cancer situation.
>
> It was originally the proposal of Senator Kennedy, and
> there was a dialog back and forth and a bill seems to
> be emerging that, to use L.B.J.'s favorite word, estab-
> lishes a "consensus" that is apparently successful and
> utilitarian from the administration's point of view and
> the committee's point of view.
>
> ...Could you think out for us, think long and hard, as
> to how we could establish some viable rapport on the
> question of greater emphasis on the problems of aging?
>
> What mechanisms, what procedures, et cetera, would in
> your judgment be workable in the framework of NIH and
> yet give some satisfaction--not complete satisfaction,
> because I don't think anything is ever complete--but
> reasonable satisfaction to this committee that a greater
> awareness and greater attention will be paid in the
> future to research relating to the aged?[25]

Marston asked whether the senator would like to have some
type of document forwarded to him, and Eagleton replied in
the same vein:

> Yes. After you have thought it out for awhile, we
> might sit down and talk it over amongst ourselves or
> something in rough document form. I would like you to
> put your good mind to work on it, and I don't question
> your sincerity, Doctor, because you are dedicated to
> this whole field of research.
>
> So I would be very interested in having your best ideas
> as to how we could place greater emphasis on this so
> that [aging research] would not be totally submerged as
> a sort of after thought, a footnote on the research
> activities of NIH.[26]

Shortly after that request, the hearings were adjourned.

BETWEEN HEARINGS

A full nine months passed before more hearings were held on the Senate bill to establish an institute on aging, but the aging issue was not dormant. The second White House Conference on Aging was held in November 1971 and members of Congress and the president took advantage of the event to promote legislation for the elderly and to keep the aging issues alive and in the public's attention. Meanwhile, the DHEW administration began to realize the seriousness of the proposed institute.

Countertactics of NIH

Marston felt that Eagleton had been impressed with the testimony of the Department of Health, Education, and Welfare, and he wanted to be responsive to the senator's request for ideas for a compromise solution to the differences in their positions, but he was also certain that Eagleton was "convinced that there was a need to undertake additional actions to insure that aging research be fostered more actively in the future."[27] Marston believed that a Center for Aging Research within NICHD would provide sufficient visibility and should be the mechanism to generate increased budgetary support for aging research.

Aware that the driving force behind Eagleton was Florence Mahoney, Marston knew that he would have to convince her that a compromise would be workable if he wanted Eagleton to consider his proposal.[28] On June 25, 1971, Marston invited Florence Mahoney to a luncheon at his home in an attempt to persuade her of his position. She was firm in her rejection of the center concept. It was too little and too late. She had been willing earlier to settle for a center and had suggested it to NIH officials, but could not get their cooperation. Now she wanted an institute. She perceived the growing support for the institute in both the House and Senate and she had watched for too long from her vantage point on the NICHD Advisory Council the lack of full support for the Gerontology Research Center in Baltimore and the failure to mount a viable extramural aging research program at NIH.[29]

After his meeting with Florence Mahoney, Marston began to "recognize the National Institute of Gerontology as a real threat."[30] On July 6 he drafted a memorandum to Kurzman warning that the upcoming White House Conference and the fact that the administration's budget proposed a $1.4 million reduction in aging research worked for the promotion of an institute. He reiterated that NIH was prepared to discuss with Eagleton the possibility of a center for aging research, but preferred "not to make this organizational change unless it were a substantial factor in decreasing the probability of a new institute."[31] Marston himself never got back to Eagleton.

1971 White House Conference

Toward the end of the interim decade, the 1960's, researchers had begun to voice their grievance to the Senate Special Committee on Aging, and a second White House Conference on Aging was proposed. A 343-page report in 1970 of the Senate Special Committee on Aging which summarized progress since the first conference and suggested issues for consideration at the upcoming second conference did not even refer to the recommendations of the first conference regarding biomedical and psychosocial aging research or the establishment of an institute.[32] At hearings before the Special Committee on Aging, Eisdorfer made a plea that in supporting service programs for the elderly, the need to establish basic information on the aging process not be neglected:

> To this end, the resolution for a forthcoming White House Conference on Aging is to be applauded, particularly if the planning for this conference includes an effort to mobilize new resources, establish improved guidelines, and focus national attention on the crucial issues at hand.[33]

Rumors circulated that President Nixon was going to kill the second White House Conference on Aging because of his experience with the Nutrition Conference, which had given him bad press. He had already shoved the Adolescence Conference out of Washington to Colorado, and was trying to move the White House Conference out of his backyard and off his back. But apparently, his efforts were too late. Nixon turned the planning of the conference over to the respected, dedicated "old war horse," Arthur Flemming. Flemming promptly took the planning out of the hands of the professionals and set up his own group, carved out of the Advisory Committee on Older Americans which had never been well staffed and had not even replaced half the members whose terms had expired. This group became the Executive Committee of the White House Conference.[34]

The 1971 White House Conference was somewhat a "grassroots" effort: 3,400 delegates met to develop national policy on

aging. This time the recommendations that emerged from the
conference were the culmination of more than 6,000 community
forums held throughout the United States in 1970. At these
community forums or "speak out" sessions, older Americans
discussed their problems fully and frankly; the conference
built its policy recommendations oń those "speak out"
sessions.

The Demand Reiterated

The second White House Conference repeated the demand of
the first White House Conference for a National Institute
of Gerontology. The Research and Demonstration Section
recommended:

> That a National Institute of Gerontology be established
> immediately to support and conduct research and training
> in the bio-medical and social-behavioral aspects of
> aging. The Institute should include study sections
> with equitable representation of the various areas
> involved in aging research and training.[35]

> The Mental Health Care Strategies and Aging Section
> recommended: that a Center for the Mental Health of
> the Aged be established within the NIMH, with the
> authority and funds for research, training, and innova-
> tive programs for older people in the community and in
> hospitals...that research monies for studies of aging
> and the elderly, from basic biological processes, to
> social and psychological phenomena, be greatly
> increased....[36]

In addition, the aging research issue now had the backing of
new advocate groups such as the National Retired Teachers
Association and the American Association of Retired Persons
which wholeheartedly supported the allocation of 5% of HEW
program funds for research and demonstration:

> To summarize, NRTA-AARP believe that the basis for
> current and future facilities and services is
> responsible Research and Demonstration and its
> judicious application....

> In light of the existing fragmented and under-financed
> approach to aging research, coupled with a rapidly
> increasing older population, The National Retired
> Teachers Association and the American Association of
> Retired Persons support an Institute of Gerontology and

a coordinated, systematic approach to Research on Aging.[37]

The discussions and recommendations at the second White House Conference on Aging clearly indicated that advocates of aging research considered the National Institute of Child Health and Human Development and the struggling Administration on Aging to be dynamics without change. Indeed, little had changed during the decade as they pursued the issue of aging research. In fact, the consensus was that aging research had less support than before the 1961 White House Conference and before the incorporation of aging research into NICHD.

Political Uses of the Conference. Clearly, an event like the White House Conference could be used for a variety of purposes by both the Congress and White House. The 1971 conference had a large base of popular support, and several of the organizations of the aged—the American Association of Retired Persons, the National Retired Teachers Association, the National Council on Senior Citizens—later became politically visible organizations.

At the conference, neither the administration nor the Congress made a case for biomedical research. Their attention was on social aspects of aging and these would become a prominent part of the legislation for the institute on aging.

President Nixon appeared at the White House Conference to announce a restoration of the budget cuts for the Administration on Aging, "and the place went into an uproar. The President seemed to be carried away with the enormous enthusiasm of the crowd"[38] as he said that he wanted the Administration on Aging budget to be increased nearly five-fold to $100 million. Although the president spoke of making Social Security benefits and Medicare benefits inflation proof, improving nursing home care services to help older people live decently in their own homes, and the need for new attitudes about aging, he said nothing about the need for any type of research on aging.

Senator Kennedy also cleverly used the impetus of the White House Conference to his advantage in aging politics. Having scheduled the vote on his bill for nutrition for the elderly during the week of the conference, Kennedy announced at the conference that the bill had passed the Senate unanimously, and he urged the administration to take action to help the elderly. Also, the conference provided Eagleton with an

opportunity to publicly endorse Kennedy's bill and thereby
gain visibility for aging issues.

In the same month the conference was convened, the Senate
Special Committee on Aging issued a working paper entitled
"Research and Training in Gerontology" which had been
prepared by the Gerontological Society at the request of
the committee. Consisting of scholarly papers contributed
by leading experts, the report covered a broad spectrum of
subjects relevant to research and training in gerontology
and provided information that would enable decision makers
to make informed judgments on policies and programs regarding aging. The paper also provided data on the number of
trained persons who could implement programs efficiently
and effectively. A sense of urgency is expressed in the
preface of the report: "Ongoing efforts in both areas
[research and training] are now threatened by actual
curtailment or by lingering uncertainty. The result is
waste of funds and the prospect of additional waste in
later attempts to 'catch up' or to remedy the mistakes of
today."[39] The report states unequivocally that public
policy on aging is based on inadequate information, and the
paper on biomedical research asserts that "a new institute
would help assure that more of the results of fundamental
biological research should be made available for the care of
patients."[40] The document not only covered the subject
in a conceptual way, but also made several recommendations
for action. To meet the need for trained personnel special-
izing in services for the aged (a need estimated at 10-15
times the level of the current level of effort), one recommendation provided that in each major region of the country
there should be at least one major interdisciplinary
training and research center, with the goal of ten centers
operating by 1982. Several recommendations for funding
were made: (1) that a minimum of $25 million be provided
for the first year of operation for a new National Institute
of Gerontology, (2) that federal funds for research and
demonstration be increased immediately to a level of 1% of
the total expenditure for health and social services for
the elderly with a gradual increase to 3% over a period of
ten years, and (3) that new money be specifically appropriated for these purposes rather than diverting present funds
from service areas.[41]

CALIFORNIA HEARINGS

The Real Issues at the California Hearings

March 1972 was a key month in the history of the legislation
to establish an institute on aging; both houses of Congress

held hearings on the institute bills. The Senate held two
days of hearings, March 3 and 4, chaired by Senator Alan
Cranston (D-CA) in San Francisco and Los Angeles on Eagleton's institute bill (S. 887) and Williams' Commission bill
(S. 1925).[42]

Cranston was a cosponsor of Eagleton's bill, but he also
had other interests in chairing the hearings in his home
state of California. He planned soon to introduce several
bills that would increase economic benefits to the elderly
under Social Security and the Administration on Aging.
During the hearings, he referred to his intended bills,
even though they were not on the agenda, and asked witnesses questions relating to them. He thereby encouraged a
discussion of social services and economic issues among the
elderly. In addition, the thirty-eight witnesses he and
his staff brought together in California represented a wide
cross-section of interests in social and service issues,
whereas the strong biomedical research interests were
largely represented at the Washington hearings.

In his opening remarks at the hearings, Cranston disclosed
that he planned to introduce amendments to the bill to
broaden the proposed scope of activities to be carried out
by the Gerontology Institute. Cranston candidly admitted
that he earlier had hesitated to cosponsor a bill for a new
institute because he questioned the advisability of any
further proliferation at NIH: "I feel at this point, however, that the Federal Government's effort in the area of
research into the process of aging must be vastly increased,
and that perhaps establishing a single, centralized agency
or commission to advance this research would create the
necessary stimulus which seems to be lacking now."[43]

Societal Issues and Action Programs. Most of the witnesses
in California did not rank gerontological research high
among their priorities and concerns. Though they did not
oppose the bill, they had a different perspective on the
proposed institute. They were more interested in social
services than in the biomedical, social, and behavioral
research and training proposed in the bill. They expressed
their reservations and solutions to the problems as they
saw them.

One witness, Mike Burk of the National League of Senior
Citizens, phrased his position directly:

> Gerontology is important, but more important is the
> establishment of a decent standard of living for our
> aged....

Research is important, but mountains of materials have
been collected by hundreds of research projects across
the Nation....I do not believe that a new project will
uncover anything new in this field. And compared with
the establishment of decent housing for the aged, the
value of a new research project pales again into insig-
nificance. Let's solve this problem before we do any
more research....Research is nice, but given the choice
between research and adequate income, there is no question which the elderly themselves would choose....[44]

The executive director of the San Francisco Home Health
Service was in favor of the proposed institute, but "not at
the expense of sensible and appropriate home health services."[45] Another witness, a nutritionist, said, "I have
been a research person for the last 10 years and I think
enough research has been done, and although we need more,
we need to channel our funds for action programs."[46]
Still another was more adamant: "We don't need any more
studies or research projects nor any more hearings of this
nature. When time has passed, these proceedings will be
historical files without any follow through action programs.
The problems of the aged will not be solved in a National
Institute of Gerontology but rather in a political arena
because that is what the National Institute is all
about."[47] Even Dr. Russel Lee, the founder of the Palo
Alto Medical Clinic and a friend that Florence Mahoney
depended on to support the legislation spoke first about
the societal issues related to aging. Although he recommended that Eagleton's bill be passed, he made it clear
that "the lack of money is the root of the troubles of the
aged."[48] Another witness was blunt about what kind of
money was needed: "What the aged need is political money
to do political things."[49]

Dr. Yung-Ping Chen, associate professor of economics,
University of California at Los Angeles, advocated that the
new institute focus on "the economic clock" concept,
particularly the economic circumstances resulting in the
decline in economic power of older persons.[50] Many comments pointed up the need to translate research findings
into useful services by dissemination of the information to
the proper people.

Scientists and the Social Sciences. A substantial amount
of the California testimony was devoted to the social and
psychological aspects of aging. Witnesses emphasized that
there really is no "older person" and that researchers need
to understand the differences among older people, what
these differences mean, and what enables individuals to
gain greater life satisfaction through mental health and

spiritual growth. Operational research including demonstration projects in the "real world" was supported.

Advocates of the behavioral sciences made a strong case for
supporting "this more diffuse area of research independent
of the competition against disease research dollars"[51]
because when aging research is expanded to include the
complexities of behavioral and social research, it tends to
be ranked further and further away on the list of priorities. Information was submitted to the subcommittee
showing that out of a total of sixty projects in aging
funded by the NICHD, only ten could be clearly identified
as being concerned with social and behavioral problems.

Russel Lee's son, Dr. Philip Lee, chancellor of the
University of California at San Francisco, former assistant
secretary for Health and Scientific Affairs in DHEW,
favored an institute with a broad mandate. He opposed the
proliferation of institutes at NIH proposed in six other
bills before the Congress at that time, but he supported an
Institute of Gerontology because it would encompass
biological, psychosocial, and clinical research. Widening
his scope to the proposed Williams bill and Cranston
amendment, Lee expressed support of both. He said the
research commission proposed in S. 1925 and the institute
are not mutually exclusive and that a number of functions
described in S. 1925 could be incorporated into a National
Institute of Gerontology. He felt that the evaluation role
that Cranston proposed should not lead to opposition to the
bill as long as such an amendment did not require that the
institute approve all research at the various federal
agencies.[52]

Dr. James Birren, director of the Ethel Percy Andrus
Gerontology Center, focused primarily on training needs,
asserting that a good bit of vital research could not be
undertaken presently because of the shortage of qualified
personnel. He urged, as he had in many forums, that
specialized centers for gerontology be established in
various parts of the country. He talked about the natural
occurrence of problems of aging in society and the
interaction between the biomedical aspects and the
social-psychological.[53]

University of Southern California biologist, Dr. Bernard
Strehler, who had helped draft the Williams bill, arrived
at a compromise in his position for the institute bill by
the time of the California hearings. He said nothing in
opposition to the social science research because he wanted
the bill to pass and felt that the broad mandate was
necessary.

Strehler opposed the administration's objection that
neither a sufficient body of information nor a sufficient
number of good scientific questions were available to
enable progress in the aging field: "...I maintain that the
information upon which this judgment was based is out of
date, that whatever the sources were, that an awareness of
the advances in molecular biology and in other aspects of
biomedicine that occurred during the last 15 years, a real
revolution, have not really been taken into account."[54]
He then listed for the committee twenty-five basic questions
challenging researchers in gerontology, and he added that
these are only a few of the basic questions awaiting
scientific research. Furthermore, he believed the questions
could be answered with presently available tools. He
pointed out that less than 25% of these problem areas were
currently under investigation by NICHD.

Strehler argued that the commission's functions specified
in the Williams bill should be a primary charge to any new
institute on aging whether those functions are a formal part
of the legislation or not: "It is precisely because no governmental body is using the expertise and fundamental scientific background available to attack these problems that a
new governmental structure is needed, either in NIH, AoA, or
elsewhere in HEW."[55] When Cranston asked Strehler whether
he favored an institute or a commission or a combination of
the two, Strehler responded candidly that because of the
institute's broader charge, "...if it is a loved child in
NIH rather than a forced adoption, then I think that such an
institute can very, very well carry out the things that need
to be done in biological and biomedical gerontology."[56]
Strehler had questioned whether the same creative dedication
applied by the NIH administration in other areas would be
applied to a new institute for aging research. His concern
was that if it were a "stepchild" institute at NIH the
situation would be far from ideal.

Some witnesses advocated caution in establishing the
proposed institute, and others articulated their reservations about more research and more studies. In order to
keep expectations at a realistic level, it was thought that
the new institute ought to avoid "grandiose programs and
unrealistic promises"[57] and that advocates of the institute ought to avoid the costly illusion that "something was
being done" simply by creating a new institute.

Clearly, the 1972 California hearings treated considerably
broader issues than the 1971 Washington Senate hearings.

Witnesses were less restricted in scope, more open and candid, and more diversified in interests. The majority of the witnesses wanted services and status for the elderly.[58] In contrast to the 1971 hearings, there was considerable sentiment against more expenditures for research and for a cautionary and prudent approach to the subject so that the public would not expect research to be the panacea for all of the problems facing older Americans.

Because of the larger, more divergent constituency represented in the California hearings, the biomedical researchers would have to begin accommodating interests other than their own immediate concerns. Unity among the advocates would be necessary to pass the bill, and that meant broadening the scope of the institute to include social and behavioral research, a scope for gerontology that the early cadre in the 1930's and 1940's had originally espoused.

CHANGES IN THE BILL

The Cranston Amendment

The pace continued in March and on March 30, 1972, Senator Cranston offered an amendment[59] to the Eagleton bill (S. 887), proposing four significant changes: to ensure training of an adequate number of allied health and paramedical personnel in the field of health care for the aged; to evaluate the psychological, physiological, and sociological aspects of aging of all federal programs for the aged; to collect and publish data related to the aging population; and to conduct public information and education programs on the problems and processes associated with growing older. Cranston pointed out that the changes would broaden the scope and focus of the proposed institute and would be consistent with his suggestion, and Eagleton's intention, to change the name of the proposed institute from the Institute of Gerontology to the Institute on Aging. It was Florence Mahoney who had originally expressed concern to Cranston and others about the need for a less technical and more popular name for the institute.[60] Cranston also mentioned that he had asked Senator Eagleton to include him as a cosponsor of S. 887. Finally, the California senator pointed out that the training function for the additional health personnel would not necessarily be carried out by the institute, but could be continued with greater visibility within the Bureau of Health Manpower Education.

Plan for Aging Research

Another change in the Senate Bill was the addition of a
section that incorporated provisions from Senator Williams'
bill (S. 1925) calling for a plan for an aging research
program. The Williams bill would have set up a separate
Aging Research Commission to develop a gerontological
research plan that would include a long-range program
designed to coordinate research of the biological, medical,
psychological, social, and economic aspects of aging. The
revised version of the Senate bill provided that the plan
would be developed within one year after the enactment of
the legislation by the secretary of HEW in consultation
with the institute and acting through the National Advisory
Council on Aging.

VOTE ON THE SENATE BILL

Although Eagleton introduced his bill (S. 887) in February
1971, and hearings were held in March and June of 1971 and
March of 1972, the Senate Committee on Labor and Public
Welfare did not report it out of Committee until June 21,
1972. The Senate bill had twenty-eight cosponsors and
almost no opposition, but the chief sponsor of the bill,
Senator Thomas Eagleton, and his staff were distracted from
legislative duties at a time when shepherding the bill and
speeding its passage were critical. This was the final
session of the 92nd Congress and if the bill did not reach
the president within ten days before adjournment of Congress, it could be killed by a pocket veto. Ordinarily, if
a bill is sent to the president and he does not sign it
within ten days, it automatically becomes law. However,
should Congress adjourn and the president retain the bill
unsigned for the ten-day period, it is automatically vetoed
and the veto cannot be overriden by Congress.

In 1972, an election year, the Democratic convention was
held in early July. Eagleton emerged as the vice-presiden-
tial candidate on the Democratic ticket with his colleague,
Senator McGovern. Although only 43 years of age, Senator
Tom Eagleton was highly regarded by the fellow legislators
and leaders within his party, but he was not well known by
rank-and-file Democrats. It was soon after this nomination
that the general public became aware of the hospitalization
and treatment for depression which the senator had suffered
in the past. The controversy surrounding that earlier
illness and the fact that Senator McGovern had not been
informed about it finally led to Eagleton's withdrawal from
the race on July 31. But the brief candidacy and the
tortuous period for Eagleton personally took time and

attention away from his legislative duties. In addition,
the chief counsel for the Senate Committee on Labor and
Public Welfare's Subcommittee on Aging, James Murphy, had
left his post to aid the senator in his campaign. The
interruption of duties probably accounts for the fact that
the institute bill was not scheduled on the Senate floor
until September, when Eagleton and his staff could get back
to the bill.

NOTES

1. Thomas Eagleton, Research in Aging and Nutrition
   Programs for the Elderly, 1971, Hearings before the
   Subcommittee on Aging of the Committee on Labor and
   Public Welfare, U.S. Senate, 92nd Congress, 1st
   Session, June 1,2,14, 1971, p. 2.

2. Harrison A. Williams, June 1971 Hearings, p. 15.

3. Nelson H. Cruikshank, June 1971 Hearings, p. 30.

4. Ibid., p. 31.

5. Ibid., p. 32.

6. Nathan Shock, interview, June 22, 1978.

7. Cyril Brickfield, June 1971 Hearings, p. 221.

8. F. Marott Sinex, June 1971 Hearings, p. 49.

9. Ibid., p. 49.

10. Ibid., p. 50.

11. Ibid., p. 52.

12. William P. Hettinger, Jr., June 1971 Hearings, p. 55.

13. Carl Eisdorfer, June 1971 Hearings, p. 79.

14. Denham Harman, June 1971 Hearings, p. 84.

15. Stephen Kurzman, June 1971 Hearings, p. 245.

16. Ibid., p. 249.

17. National Institute on Aging, Report (S. 887) No.
    92-1134, Senate, 92nd Congress, 2nd Session, September
    1972, p. 4.

18. Kurzman, June 1971 Hearings, p. 249.

19. Report No. 92-1134, p. 5.

20. Kurzman, June 1971 Hearings, p. 253.

21. Gerald LaVeck, June 1971 Hearings, p. 274.

22. Eagleton, June 1971 Hearings, p. 285.

23. Robert Marston, June 1971 Hearings, p. 285.

24. Ibid., p. 288.

25. Eagleton, June 1971 Hearings, p. 289.

26. Ibid.

27. Robert Marston draft of memo to assistant secretary for Legislation, NIH, July 6, 1971, p. 1.

28. Robert Marston, interview, May 14, 1978.

29. Florence Mahoney, interview, May 15, 1979.

30. Marston, memo, p. 2.

31. Ibid., p. 3.

32. Developments in Aging 1970, a Report of the Special Committee on Aging, United States Senate, February 16, 1970.

33. Carl Eisdorfer, "Patterns of Federal Funding for Research in Aging," The Gerontologist, 8 (1967-68): 6.

34. Toward a National Policy on Aging, Proceedings of the 1971 White House Conference on Aging, vol. 2.

35. 1971 White House Conference on Aging: A Report to the Delegates from the Conference Sections and Special Concerns Sessions, Senate Document No. 92-53, December 1971 (Washington, D.C.: GPO, 1971), p. 47.

36. Ibid., pp. 72-73.

NIMH established the Center for Studies of the Mental Health of the Aging (CSMHA) in 1975. The Center's role is to examine mental health issues and problems from the perspective of an interplay of research, services, and training. What began as a coordinating center for

NIMH centers evolved to one with funding capacities. CSMHA started its operations with an intensive period of planning, involving the whole of NIMH, other federal agencies, and a significant number of consultants from the field.

37. Proposals for a National Policy on Aging: Policy Statement (Washington, D.C.: NTRA and AARP, 1971), pp. 61-63.

38. Carl Eisdorfer interview, July 10, 1978.

    FY 1971 funding: $32 million; administrative request for FY 1972, $29.5 million; later FY 1972 appropriation $44.75 million, or $15.25 million more than the budget request. Acting on a supplemental appropriation bill later in December, the House and Senate increased the appropriation to $100 million.

39. Frank Church, "Preface," Research and Training in Gerontology, Special Committee on Aging: U.S. Senate (Washington, D.C.: GPO, 1971), p. iii.

40. F. Marott Sinex, in "Introduction and Summary of Parts," Research and Training, p. 2.

41. James E. Birren and Kathy Gribbin, in "Introduction," Research and Training, pp. 3-4, and paper by Gerontological Society, p. 56.

42. A third institute bill, submitted by Frank E. Moss (D-UT) was also on the agenda.

43. Alan Cranston, Research in Aging, 1972, Hearings before the Subcommittee on Aging of the Committee on Labor and Public Welfare, United States Senate, 92nd Congress, 2nd Session, March 3-4, 1972, p. 1.

44. Mike Burk, March 1972 Hearings, pp. 187-189.

45. Hadley Hall, March 1972 Hearings, p. 71.

46. Nylda Gemple, March 1972 Hearings, p. 94.

47. Charles Clay, March 1972 Hearings, p. 104.

48. Russel Lee, March 1972 Hearings, p. 59.

49. Clay, Ibid, p. 115.

50. Yung-Ping Chen, March 1972 Hearings, p. 200.

51. Robert Nathan, March 1972 Hearings, p. 180.

52. Philip Lee, March 1972 Hearings, pp. 64-67.

53. James Birren, March 1972 Hearings, p. 147.

54. Bernard Strehler, March 1972 Hearings, p. 170.

55. Ibid., p. 172.

56. Ibid., p. 186.

57. Roger Cornut, March 1972 Hearings, p. 79.

58. A careful analytic observation was introduced in the
    hearing when Mr. Louis Kuplan, a private consultant on
    retirement planning and the problems of aging, pointed
    out questionable wording in the Williams bill.   He
    indicated that Section 2 of S. 1925 states that "The
    Congress hereby finds and declares, that the aging
    process usually results in the gradual deterioration of
    memory,   certain   aspects   of   learning...."   Kuplan
    strongly urged that this sentence be reworded because
    it cannot be substantiated by scientific findings and
    "is an outgrowth of old myths, commonly held belief,
    that you can't teach an old dog new tricks.   This
    concept has done more harm to learning in later life
    than   any   other   concept.   It   creates   mental   and
    emotional   blocks   to   learning   in   later   life....I
    recommend that you change this wording so that the
    Congress will not be in the position of helping to
    perpetuate such a misleading concept of the mental
    abilities of older Americans."   Kuplan's advice to
    delete the phrase was heeded when portions of S. 1925
    were later incorporated into the revised bill to create
    an institute.

59. Kuplan, March 1972 Hearings, p. 83.

60. Alan Cranston, Congressional Record-Senate, March 30,
    1972, p. 11070.   F. Marott Sinex and Florence Mahoney,
    telephone conversations, November 23, 1979.

7
Getting the House Bill Passed

Simultaneous to convincing senators to introduce and pass a bill for an institute, Florence Mahoney and other forces were at work on the House side. Initially, the House bill proposed a more restricted mandate for the institute than had the Senate bill. Only biomedical research was called for. Later, as the informal coalition of forces supporting the bill sought to satisfy all interests and assure passage of the bill, ill-fated changes were made in a compromising spirit, in particular, an add-on to provide mental health services for the elderly by amending the Community Health Centers Act.

Less than two weeks after the California Senate hearings, the House began hearings on three bills that proposed establishing a National Institute of Gerontology.

INTRODUCING THE BILLS

Florence Mahoney personally visited several of her friends in the House and enlisted their support for the bill. She documented her position with facts about meager funds, inadequate staff, and the potential for biomedical research breakthroughs on the aging process. She brought in a few influential lay persons and knowledgeable researchers to meet informally with key members of Congress.

Furthermore, she went directly to the congressman with
clout--Paul Rogers, chairman of the Subcommittee on Public
Health and Environment of the House Interstate and Foreign
Commerce Committee. A Democrat from Florence Mahoney's
home state of Florida, Rogers knew and respected her from
her earlier efforts to get support for biomedical research
at NIH; he and his staff referred to her affectionately as
"Flo Mo."

Rogers was informed and already committed to support for
biomedical research. He was not concerned about the
proliferation of institutes at NIH, and had supported the
establishment of the National Eye Institute in 1968.
Citing the constantly low level of funding for aging
research at NICHD, Florence Mahoney convinced Rogers that
an institute for aging research was the only way to get
federal funding and a focus on gerontology.[1] She used
the National Eye Institute as an example of how a separate
entity within NIH generates support.

Behind the scenes, Florence Mahoney gained the wholehearted
support not only of Rogers but also of the chairman of the
full Interstate and Foreign Commerce Committee, Harley O.
Staggers (D-WVA). Staggers had been advised by Lee S.
Hyde, a young physician on the committee staff, that
another institute would be an "irrational institute
structure" and poor management policy; but, after talking
with her, Staggers instructed Hyde that "Mrs. Mahoney is a
wonderful woman and should be helped with this bill--do
it!"[2]

Meanwhile, once again, Springer had introduced another bill
for aging research, H.R. 3336, which this time got on the
formal agenda.

                    HEARINGS ON THE HOUSE BILL

Hearings in the House were held on March 14-16, 1972, by
the Subcommittee on Public Health and Environment on bills
to establish an institute for aging research: Springer's
bill (H.R. 3336), Rogers' bill (H.R. 12308), and seven other
bills.[3] Only the Rogers bill received serious consideration
at the hearings.

In both the Rogers and Springer bills, the focus was still
on biomedical research, with no mention of the social or
behavioral sciences, as was preferred by Florence Mahoney,
biomedical researchers, and numerous other advocates.
However, there were several important differences between

the two bills. In Rogers' bill, for the first time, the proposed institute was referred to as a National Institute of Aging, not of Gerontology or Geriatrics. Florence Mahoney had suggested that change to Rogers (and to Cranston) because "nobody knows what 'gerontology' is"[4] and the term "aging" would have much wider appeal than the more scientific term. A second difference she encouraged was in the mandate of the institute. Springer's bill called for research on the treatments and cures for diseases of the aged whereas Rogers' bill would support research of the aging process and preventive measures with respect to the special health problems of the aged. This move from the disease focus to a study of the process of aging was a major modification. A third major addition in the Rogers bill was the inclusion of a section to amend the Community Mental Health Centers Act to provide grants for the construction of facilities to provide mental health services for the elderly. A bill with similar provisions was before the Senate, and the White House Conference had called for such support. Mrs. Mahoney and her colleagues were not happy about this addition to the institute bill because it was an "add-on" not related to the institute itself and opposition to it could kill the entire bill. On the other hand, the add-on attracted the attention of many legislators.

In these hearings and throughout the legislative process, Chairman Rogers linked humanitarian concerns with the practical aspects of governmental and political necessity. He spoke of the opportunity before Congress to combine doing something to make human life more significant with doing something that would result in economic savings on the cost of health care for the elderly.

The Administration's Position

The leading administration witness was Dr. Merlin DuVal, the assistant secretary for Health and Scientific Affairs, DHEW, accompanied by several colleagues, including Dr. Gerald LaVeck, director of the National Institute of Child Health and Human Development. After presenting estimates of government expenditures for health care of the aged in 1973 ($11.7 billion by the federal government), DuVal stated the reasons for the Administration's strenuous objection to the establishment of the proposed institute: (1) no mere organization change can cause a research area to flourish, (2) administrative costs would be at the expense of other high-priority health areas, and (3) separating out aging research would cause duplication.

According to DuVal, the administration shared the objective
of the subcommittee to upgrade the priority of aging
research; the difference was in the mechanism for achieving
the objective. DuVal talked on behalf of a center for aging
research, the concept Marston had proposed to Florence
Mahoney as an alternative to an institute. DuVal described
the center as a coordinating supervisory office with authority to give extramural grants and contracts, especially in
developing multidisciplinary research at universities and
other institutes.[5]

Saying that everything in Rogers' bill could be accomplished
under existing authority, the assistant secretary was
evasive in responding to Congressman Hastings' question
about whether additional resources are needed within the
existing structure: "...the issue of additional resources
is where Solomon-type judgment must be made," replied DuVal.
The questioning persisted, "Is it true that aging research
has not been given the same support that child health
research has?" DuVal answered, "In dollars that is true.
In proportions, it is not true. As a matter of fact, since
we started in 1965, the growth in the budget for aging is
approximately 270 percent, greatly outstripping the investment growth in child health. But in dollars, we provide at
this time more dollars for child development."[6]

Chairman Rogers then engaged in a pointed discussion with
DuVal and LaVeck.[7] Rogers had several concerns, among
them the apparent effort to keep aging research expenditures at 11% of the NICHD budget and the underutilization
of the Baltimore Center. Rogers pushed LaVeck to a "professional judgment" regarding the budget NICHD could adequately
use for aging research, and LaVeck reluctantly indicated
that "$4 million would be a rough estimate over the next 2
years."[8] LaVeck added that the scientific community had
not been overwhelmingly excited about research in the aging
area and that although NICHD has a record of trying to
stimulate them, "the number of proposals, for example, that
we received last year that related to aging, was only 103
for the entire Institute."[9] In response to Rogers'
question about bringing the Baltimore Center to full
capacity for proper use, LaVeck gave a vague response of
"We certainly hope over the years to do so." Impatient,
Rogers quipped, "We all hope over the years, but have you
got any plans to bring it to proper use?"[10] Rogers'
question about research areas would be heard many times
before the new legislation was in place: "What are the
most promising areas of research that you are now going

into?" The administration cited aging in women; immunology and aging; cellular programming and aging, particularly studies of DNA and RNA; nutritional and environmental factors in aging; and social aspects of aging.[11]

Positions of the Professional Communities

Dr. Bernard Strehler testified before the House subcommittee. As he had done in California at the Senate hearings, Strehler directly countered the administration's key arguments. He alluded to the support expressed by the major professional organizations and said that he found the president's speech at the end of the 1971 White House Conference "a little strange" in that it omitted any mention of the importance of research, especially since "research is an investment in the future and this administration certainly believes in the wisdom of investment...."[12] Strehler confessed that if there was proper funding, he would have no problem with keeping the aging program at NICHD; but, he said, that was not the case—aging is funded at only 50% of the level of fifteen years ago. Strehler gave three major reasons for a National Institute on Aging: the underutilization of the Baltimore Center, the limited available funds, and a lack of advocacy for aging at the higher administrative levels of NIH.[13]

Dr. Ewald W. Busse, a well-known leader in the field of gerontology from Duke University School of Medicine, testified as president of the American Psychiatric Association (APA). Busse said he was particularly pleased that Rogers' bill called for research on prevention and that the Community Mental Health Centers provisions which Rogers had added were critical to research and training needs.[14]

Virginia Stone from the Geriatric Nursing Practice Division of the American Nurses' Association (ANA) and Director of the Graduate School of Nursing at Duke University spoke for the application of research to nursing practice. She recommended research in the areas of genetics, nutrition, physiology, endocrinology, psychiatry, cultural influences, and common health concerns of the aged such as incontinence, disorientation, and the use of multiple drugs. The ANA recommended that if a National Advisory Council on Aging were formed it should be multidisciplinary and that qualified nurse researchers in fields related to gerontology should be appointed to the council.[15]

The representative of the Council for Social Research in Aging discussed examples of the relevancy of social-behavioral aspects and urged that the kind of language found in S. 887 (Eagleton's bill) be used since it specified medical, social, and behavioral research at the proposed institute.[16] The executive director of the National Council of Senior Citizens emphasized quality of life: "We are not advocating unlimited longevity. We realize that much of this research that we support would not benefit those of us who are now senior citizens, but rather we are working for the benefit of our children and grandchildren. We want to help create a better life for those who are aged rather than prolong life indefinitely."[17] The American Dental Hygienists Association sent a letter in support of H.R. 12308 to Congressman Rogers on March 27, 1972.

The only professional organization expressing a strong formal objection to the bill was the Association of American Medical Colleges (AAMC). Dr. John A. Cooper, president of the AAMC, wrote a letter to Congressman Rogers the last day of hearings stating the association's opposition to the bill. (A year later he would send an identical letter to Rogers just prior to the hearings held on March 16, 1973.) In the letter Cooper expressed two major concerns about the bill. First, he hoped that the subcommittee was making a clear distinction between the scientific research problems of understanding the aging process and the economic problems of the aged represented by the need for medical care and other services. Second, he felt that there is a paucity of trained researchers and valid ideas in the field of aging research and that the mere establishment of a national institute on aging would not mean that scientists would be on the verge of discovering ways to modify the aging process or to postpone death.[18] Ethel Shanas, president of the Gerontological Society, and other society officials visited Cooper in an attempt to change the AAMC's position, but their argument met with firm rejection.

The American Dental Association (ADA) also sent a letter to Rogers, but its position was less firm than that of the AAMC. The ADA did not want to oppose the bill, but preferred that the funding go to the National Institute of Dental Research.[19]

And finally, one scientific organization lobbied against the creation of an institute although it never submitted testimony at any of the hearings. Instead, the Public Affairs Committee (PAC) of the Federation of American Societies for Experimental Biology (FASEB) resolved to

approach Senator Eagleton. PAC spoke only for itself, not
for the federation which never took a formal or written
position.[20] A well-known and highly respected biologist,
who was chairman of the Biological Sciences Division of the
Gerontological Society, had made efforts to neutralize the
federation's opposition to the bill.

At the close of the hearings on March 16, Florence Mahoney
made a statement, the only one by her ever recorded in the
hearings related to the bill. Although she attended all of
the hearings and coached witnesses for hours prior to their
testimony, she preferred to stay in the background; but
Rogers would not let her presence go unnoticed:

> I would like to note the presence of Mrs. Florence
> Mahoney who has been sitting through all of the hear-
> ings, and who has been a driving force in the country
> for programs to aid in the solution of the problems in
> aging.
>
> This committee is very much aware of her efforts, and
> she can claim a great deal of credit for all of this
> work that is going on in trying to do something about
> the problems associated with aging.
>
> I don't know whether you would like to say something to
> the committee or not, Mrs. Mahoney?

Her response was simply: "I would like just to thank you
because I think that the testimony has been very, very
important, and to the point."[21]

A CLEAN BILL: OUT OF COMMITTEE

After hearings and other deliberations, a subcommittee
typically drafts a single "clean bill" to send to its
committee for consideration. As a courtesy to Springer who
had introduced the first bill for an institute, and out of
political expediency to that Republican, Chairman Rogers
requested Springer to introduce the "clean bill" to the
Subcommittee on Public Health and Environment. Rogers'
staff drafted the bill, H.R. 14424, and Springer introduced
it on April 1, 1972. It was referred to the Committee on
Interstate and Foreign Commerce ten days later, passed by a
voice vote, and reported for scheduling of debate on the
House calendar.

No amendments were offered to the bill during committee
consideration. A budget was not proposed because, as the
committee report accompanying H.R. 14424 states:

The costs associated with the establishment of a new
institute cannot be ascertained, since no new authority
is granted to the National Institutes of Health by the
legislation. The bill merely consolidates the authority
of a variety of institutes, primarily the National
Institute of Child Health and Human Development, which
relate to the aging process and problems of the aged,
into a new institute.[22]

Regarding coordination of aging research and programs, the
report explains that the Advisory Council established by
the legislation

> ...is also given the duty of advising, consulting with,
> and making recommendations to the Secretary on all
> programs relating to aged which are administered by him.
> The Council shall also monitor such programs and the
> programs conducted by the Institute, and submit to the
> President annually for transmittal to the Congress an
> evaluation of the efficacy of such programs, together
> with recommendations for improvements.[23]

VOTE ON THE HOUSE BILL

Rogers sped his bill through the House from hearings in
mid-March of 1972 to passage in the House by mid-July.
House debate on the institute bill was scheduled on July
18, 1972, and Chairman Staggers, Committee on Interstate
and Foreign Commerce, introduced it to the chamber.
Staggers paid tribute to Springer, crediting him with
introducing this bill in 1960 and "in every subsequent
Congress. And the 1971 White House Conference recommended
to the Congress exactly what Mr. Springer had been recommending for the past 12 years."[24] After advocating
passage of the bill, Staggers gave the floor to Springer,
whose introductory remarks recounted the main points of the
legislative history to that point, emphasizing that there
simply was not enough money being spent by NIH for aging
research and that the nation needed to understand considerably more about the causes of human aging.

Rogers spoke in support of the bill, emphasizing that the
bill is not so much intended to extend life as it is to
make life healthier and that the bill will result in
savings from not having to put so many people into nursing
homes. Saying that by creating the National Institute of
Child Health and Human Development in 1964 the Congress had
ignored the 1961 White House Conference recommendation for
a National Institute of Gerontology, Rogers continued:

"Last year, the White House Conference on Aging evaluated the efficacy of this decision." He explained that dele- gates representing every state gave priority recommendation through the conference sections of aging research and demonstration to establish a National Institute of Geron- tology, a recommendation affirmed by other conference sections—the training section, special concerns section, and the section on aged blacks, as well as the section on physical and mental health which rendered a strong sugges- tion that the new institute be established. Ending his remarks optimistically, Rogers stated: "There are con- vincing reasons to believe that creation of a separate institute...will add years, perhaps decades, of additional health in the middle years." Rogers again credited "one person who has been a constant promoter of research on aging and who has urged that Congress take this action—Mrs. Florence Mahoney who has done a magnificent job on bringing the need for this Institute to the attention of this commit- tee and to the attention of the Congress."[25]

No actual debate on the bill took place. A clarification was made between the functions of the National Advisors Council on Aging proposed in S. 887 and those of the National Advisory Council on Aging established in the Older Americans Act (H.R. 1), passed by the House the day before. The former would deal with the scientific aspects of research and training and the Older Americans Council would advise the president on matters dealing primarily with benefit and tax programs for the elderly.

The praise on the House floor was almost unanimous—only one vote raised a momentary, questioning note. Foreseeing the raising of that "institutional" voice, Springer, in his introductory remarks, challenged: "I do not think even my distinguished colleague from Iowa is going to object to this bill when I get through talking to him about it and about the cost."[26] The "institutional" and "distin- guished" voice from Iowa was Republican H. R. Gross, whose voice had been raised many times over the years on behalf of federal economy and against government spending. Gross was not to disappoint his colleagues this time: "...we do not need to spend millions of dollars, so far as I am concerned, to tell me that I am getting older as the days go by. There are other things that tell me that, and some of them I regret very much. I just do not know—I'm still unconvinced that this bill is necessary."[27]

At the conclusion of the debate, the House of Representa- tives overwhelmingly adopted the bill—yeas 380, nays 10, not voting 42. Perhaps the actions of the House that week were best captured by Congressman William Randall (D-MO) who had chaired the Special Study Subcommittee on the Problems of the Aging (1971-1972):

> ...the legislative week that began yesterday may well be reported in the future as the week that the U.S. House of Representatives took the time to write into law some of the things that have so very long been needed to benefit our senior citizens.
>
> It will be recalled that yesterday the House passed some important amendments extending and improving the Older Americans Act H.R. 15657....
>
> Now today, Mr. Chairman, on the second day of this legislative week we are about to make yet another advance for our older citizens as we vote to establish a National Institute of the Aging.[28]

NOTES

1. Florence Mahoney, interview, May 15, 1979.

2. Lee Hyde, interview, May 31, 1978.

3. Bertman Podell's (D-NY) bill (H.R. 13975) and six bills identical to Springer's bill.

   All eight members, except John G. Schmitz of California, of the Subcommittee on Public Health and Environment joined Rogers in cosponsoring H.R. 12308.

4. Mahoney interview, May 15, 1979.

5. Merlin K. DuVal, National Institute of Aging, Hearings before the Subcommittee on Public Health and Environment of the Committee on Interstate and Foreign Commerce, House of Representatives, 92nd Congress, 2nd Session, March 14-16, 1972 (Washington, D.C.: GPO, 1972), p. 21.

6. Ibid., pp. 23-25.

7. Ibid., pp. 24, 25-26.

8. Gerald LaVeck, March 1972 Hearings, p. 44.

9. Ibid., p. 44. In 1969, 103 of 8,603 proposals submitted to NICHD were for aging research (March 1972 Hearings, p. 126).

10. Ibid., p. 47.

11. Rogers, DuVal, and LaVeck, March 1972 Hearings, pp. 37-42.

12. Bernard Strehler, March 1972 Hearings, p. 79.

13. Ibid., p. 78.

14. Ewald W. Busse, March 1972 Hearings, pp. 72-75. In August 1974, after the bill had become law, Busse testified before the Senate as president-elect of the American Geriatrics Society along with its president, Robert B. Greenblatt.

15. Virginia Stone, March 1972 Hearings, pp. 92-94.

16. Warren A. Peterson, March 1972 Hearings, p. 120.

17. William R. Hutton, March 1972 Hearings, p. 105.

18. John A. D. Cooper, March 1972 Hearings, pp. 144-145.

19. Carl A. Laughlin, March 1972 Hearings, p. 146:

> The various provisions of H.R. 12308 seem to us to be, in themselves, well-designed to intensify attention--both with respect to basic and applied research--to the health problems of the aged. Whether it is necessary to establish a National Institute of Aging in order to carry out this program, is, we think, more problematical....
>
> Before final action is taken on H.R. 12308, we would hope that intensive consideration could be given to accomplishing the proposal's laudable aims by special funding of existing institutes. The National Institute of Dental Research, as an example, would be in an excellent position, with appropriate funding, to undertake programs relating to the oral health needs of the aged.

20. The following resolution is recorded in the March 1973 (PAC) minutes:

> After considerable discussion of the bill, the Public Affairs Committee decided the best approach was to suggest to Senator Eagleton that the name of the NICHD be changed to embrace "aging" and additional funds be included in the appropriation for NICHD for research and training. The committee

took this position in view of the total budget situation relative to the support of research at NIH and because the proliferation of current institute responsibilities would cost sizable additional monies, which at this time are not likely to be appropriated.

In a letter dated February 20, 1974 to Dr. Leonard Hayflick, chairman of the Biological Sciences Division of the Gerontological Society, the chairman of PAC explained the committee's position:

> ...on about five or six occasions the Committee discussed the proposed legislation for the establishment of a new institute. We are entirely sympathetic with the importance of the field, and we recognize that it has not received the kind of interest which it needs. At the same time we were convinced that the climate for the establishment of a new institute of NIH was exceedingly uncertain and likely to be negative.

> Our conclusion...is that a separate institute not be established at this time, but that every effort be made to expand the NICHD program so that Human Development may properly include Aging, which is certainly a part of it.

> We communicated this thought to Senator Eagleton. There was considerable discussion about a possible change for NICHD to include aging. Such discussions usually led to the fact that there are and would be pushes for other institutes such as population, nutrition and others.

In the minutes of a May 8, 1974 PAC meeting, additional and somewhat different reasons were given for the Committee's opposition:

> The PAC in 1972 opposed the establishment of an NIA on the basis that research on aging cannot be separated from research performed in other Institutes. There is a question as to whether funds would be taken away from other Institutes to support an NIA. The Committee considers the proliferation of Institutes undesirable. No further action was considered necessary at this time.

From a letter to the author from Ms. Ann Nixon, executive Assistant of the Federation of American Societies for Experimental Biology, December 31, 1979.

21. Paul Rogers and Florence Mahoney, March 1972 Hearings, pp. 143-144.

22. National Institute of Aging, Report No. 92-1026 on H.R. 14424, 92nd Congress, 2nd Session, April 27, 1972, p. 2.

23. Ibid., p. 5.

24. Neither a search of the United States House of Representatives Committee on Interstate and Foreign Commerce Committee calendar from 1958 to 1961 nor a search of the Congressional Record for that same period located any documentation of submission of a bill by Springer prior to December 9, 1969. Information from interviews with Rogers, Springer, and Kenneth J. Painter (who has been on the committee staff since 1952 and is staff director and chief clerk of the committee) indicates that statements by Staggers and Rogers regarding an introduction of the bill prior to that time were probably based on inaccurate recollection of dates. Springer himself at the House hearings only claimed to have introduced it for five subsequent years: "I have long been a supporter of the establishment of a National Institute for the Aging. I have introduced a bill in each one of the last 5 years in support of that legislation." (William Springer, Hearings before the Subcommittee on Public Health and Environment, 92nd Congress, 2nd Session, on H.R. 12308 and other bills, March 14-16, 1972, p. 73.)

25. Paul Rogers, Congressional Record-House, July 18, 1972, p. 24124-24125.

26. H. R. Gross, C.R. July 18, 1972, p. 24124.

27. William Randall, C.R. July 18, 1972, pp. 24127-28.

Randall chaired the Special Study Subcommittee on Problems of the Aging which existed from 1971-1972. The Committee Reform Amendments of 1974 (H. Res. 988) rearranged committees H. Res. 988 and established the Select Committee on Aging. On February 6, 1975 Bill Randall was appointed 1st chairman of the committee.

8
Passage and a Presidential Message

After the process of writing, debating, and amending the bill into language acceptable to Congress, and given the unanimous, bipartisan support of the bill, no one in Congress seemed to expect the president's reaction. Yet, in retrospect, the administration's position and strategy of opposition seem obvious. Although the president and DHEW were making statements supportive of meeting the problems of the elderly, they were proposing different structural mechanisms for achieving their goals. They did not have an institute in mind. The more the administration perceived the institute concept to be a real threat, the more carefully the president and NIH timed their efforts and messages to be strategic.

COUNTERTACTICS OF THE ADMINISTRATION

A Message from the President

Precisely one week after the conclusion of the House hearings in March 1972, Nixon delivered a formal message to Congress transmitting recommendations for action on behalf of older Americans. The message was well timed politically. The unmet needs of the elderly were gaining even more visibility, and now interest groups on behalf of the elderly were increasing rapidly. The second White House Conference

on Aging had concluded less than four months earlier. In
Congress, proposals to amend the Social Security Act (H.R.
1) and to establish an institute for aging research were
under consideration. Furthermore, 1972 was an election
year, with a Democratic Congress and a Republican president.

Perhaps seeking to establish his leadership among the
elderly, Nixon highlighted specific steps his administration
had taken to implement a structure for what he called a
"comprehensive strategy for meeting the complex problems"
of the aged. In 1969, he recalled, he established a special
Task Force on Aging and elevated the commissioner on Aging
to the position of special assistant to the president on
Aging, the first such position in history. Later, he
created a new Cabinet-level Committee on Aging under the
leadership of the secretary of Health, Education, and
Welfare. After convening the White House Conference on
Aging, he asked the Cabinet-level Committee on Aging to
place the recommendation of the conference at the top of
its agenda and he asked the chairman of the conference,
Arthur Flemming, to stay on as special consultant to the
president on Aging. The president disclosed more structural
plans for the future. The secretary of Health, Education,
and Welfare would strengthen the department's Advisory
Committee on Older Americans and increase its staff to meet
its responsibilities. The Commissioner of Aging, in his
capacity as chairman of the Advisory Committee, would report
directly to the secretary.

The emphasis of the president's message was clearly on
services and economics, with the latter discussed under
sections of the message entitled "Where the Money Comes
From" and "Where the Money Goes." Nixon also addressed the
issue of government research activities on the process and
problems of aging:

> What we need is a comprehensive, coordinated research
> program, one which includes disciplines ranging from
> biomedical research to transportation systems analysis,
> from psychology and sociology to management science and
> economics. To coordinate the development of such a
> program, a new Technical Advisory Committee for Aging
> Research will be created in the office of the Secretary
> of Health, Education, and Welfare.[1]

Anyone reading these words of the president in late March
could easily have surmised that the president would be
receptive to the proposed idea of an institute for research
on aging. Few, if any, congressmen understood the exclu-
sivity of the words.

TACAR

Seasoned politicians are well aware of the adage, "You
can't beat something with nothin'." The administration's
establishment of a Technical Advisory Committee on Aging
Research (TACAR) in 1972 is best explained by that adage.
In announcing the establishment of TACAR, DHEW Secretary
Elliott Richardson emphasized the appropriateness of
locating the committee in the Office of the Secretary
because of its charge to develop a comprehensive plan for
the various research activities conducted by HEW. In a
memorandum, location in the Administration on Aging was
discounted, "given the arguments of visibility and access
that have been made on this issue."[2] Therefore, the
staffs not only of TACAR but also of the Advisory Committee
on Older Americans were assigned to different units of the
Office of the Secretary.

Authority for TACAR came from Executive Order 11007 with
the mandate to make recommendations to the secretary
concerning ways to better coordinate and expedite
departmental efforts in support of aging research, both
biomedical and psychosocial.[3] The committee was to
terminate two years from the date of establishment unless
an extension was requested and approved. TACAR would
report no less frequently than once a year to the
secretary, and would be composed of eighteen nonfederal
employees.

On June 6, 1972, Secretary Richardson announced the
appointment of sixteen members of the newly formed
committee, describing the formation of the committee as a
"major advance in the efforts of this Department to better
serve the needs and interests of our older citizens."[4]
About a week later, a Memorandum of Understanding was
proposed within the department, laying out the working
arrangement between TACAR and the Older American Advisory
Committee on Aging Research, since it appeared that both
groups had very similar responsibilities.

At the first meeting on October 10, 1972, Richardson
announced that:

> Since the creation of the Technical Advisory Committee,
> the House and Senate have passed bills to create a
> National Institute on Aging....
>
> The legislation would mandate the creation of a
> 16-member Advisory Council for the new institute--with
> responsibilities which would overlap, to a very

significant extent, those which I had intended for your committee.

It is, therefore, my present intention—upon enactment of the new legislation—formally to disband the Technical Advisory Committee on Aging Research; to look to the new Council for the continuing advice which your Committee would have provided; and to look—although not exclusively so—to the members of this Committee for the membership of the new Council.[5]

Apparently, Richardson, like everyone else, expected Nixon to sign the bill, or else he anticipated that Congress would override a veto. TACAR was dissolved in 1974 when the National Institute on Aging was established by law. TACAR's abrupt dissolution gives credence to the idea that it was there simply to head off the legislation. Senator Church, a member of the Senate Special Committee on Aging, is quoted as saying: "The scope of this committee [TACAR] is left very much in doubt, however, and there is no indication that it will have much power outside its role as a coordinator."[6]

NIH: Maintaining the Status Quo

At NIH, efforts to counter the persistent efforts to establish a new institute fell to Dr. Marston, the director. The Administration's reluctance to expand aging research had a long history. The NIH Gerontological Center in Baltimore had been understaffed and underfunded since its creation in 1940. The NIH Center for Aging Research in the 1950's without resources had been no more than a buffer to deter researchers seeking gerontological research support. The NICHD Center on Aging in the 1960's and early 1970's was a low budget priority and was cut back when the Family Planning Center was enhanced. Yet, in retrospect, Marston reflects that "If the Congress had felt that the Administration was putting in the necessary dollars, we probably would not have had an institute."[7]

In the summer of 1972, NIH began covering all bases and gearing up for either a veto message or legislation establishing an institute.[8] Dr. John Sherman, Marston's deputy director, refuted "hard line" talk at NIH about just ignoring the "inevitable legislation" and decided that NIH should move ahead with plans for implementation. He believed that if NIH took a rigid position of not implementing the pending legislation, control could slip out of their hands and nobody would know what might happen later.

His view was that if there was to be a National Institute on
Aging, it should be the best National Institute on Aging
within the framework of the NIH.[9] In his August 22, 1972,
memo he discussed the scope of the new institute and said
that it was agreed that "we should resist efforts to extend
the programs of the Institute to a service type responsibility reflected, for example, in an array of activities
comprising the Mental Health Institute programs."[10]
Sherman had contacted Florence Mahoney, who agreed with him
that the capabilities and resources of a new institute
should not be dissipated in other than research activities.
They then discussed the names of some individuals who might
be considered for the directorship of the new institute.

THE FINAL VERSION

Having passed companion bills to establish an institute on
aging, the House and Senate had the final task of arriving
at a single approved bill. A final version was easily
produced in October. Both houses of Congress accommodated
each other in writing amendments, and four substantive
differences[11] between the bills were settled. First, the
Senate amendment spelled out in some detail the structure
and membership of an advisory council to the institute
whereas the House bill provided for such an advisory council
in general terms. In the final version, the advisory committee structure was retained as provided in the original
House bill, with representation for social scientists along
with biomedical scientists and public representatives.
Second, the House bill specified only biomedical research
whereas the Senate bill provided for social and behavioral
research as well. The language in the Senate bill on
biomedical, social, and behavioral research was retained.
Third, the Senate amendment called for the development of
the aging research plan which had been a major part of the
Williams bill, but was not contained in the House bill.
The plan was included. Fourth, the House bill contained an
amendment to the Community Mental Health Centers program to
establish a special emphasis program for mental health
services for the elderly. This amendment was retained in
the bill.

When the Senate was considering the final version on
October 12, the only Senator to speak other than Eagleton
was Senator Glenn Beall (R-MD), the ranking minority member
of the Subcommittee on Aging. Beall voiced his support for
a coordinated research program that is capable of "system-
atically unlocking the secrets of the aging process" and
explained his support for the new institute: "...I believe
that the health and welfare of millions of older Americans

will be, over a period of time, substantially improved as a
result of the research conducted by the National Institute
on Aging."[12] Beall's support for the bill was a hard
blow for officials from the NIH who had personally lobbied
him as the ranking Republican on the Committee, with the
hope that he would oppose the bill. Beall's statement is
particularly interesting in that passage of the bill was
already assured.

In closing, Senator Eagleton praised Florence Mahoney:

> ...I cannot let this opportunity pass without paying
> tribute to a very distinguished lady, Mrs. Florence
> Mahoney...whose intelligence, determination, and con-
> cern for the creation of a National Institute on Aging
> contributed in a very large measure to the enactment of
> this legislation. Indeed...were it not contrary to the
> accepted practice, I would suggest that the new insti-
> tute might appropriately be known as the Florence
> Mahoney Institute on Aging--her role has been of that
> great a significance....While I did not presume to
> intrude on the prerogatives of the Secretary of Health,
> Education, and Welfare, I strongly commend Mrs. Mahoney
> to him with the hope that he may find her to be a
> suitable nominee for a position on the advisory council
> in the new institute.[13]

Mrs. Mahoney served on the National Advisory Council on
Aging from its creation until October 31, 1978.

Congress passed the final version of H.R. 14424 on October
14, 1972, and sent it to the president for approval on
October 17, just one day before the Congress adjourned. The
next day President Nixon's memorandum of disapproval--ef-
fecting a pocket veto--was published in the Congressional
Record.

A POCKET VETO

The president's veto of H.R. 14424 was not expected. Even
though the administration had opposed the bill at hearings,
it was expected that the president would sign a bill so
unanimously supported by Congress in an election year. The
president's Science Advisor, Dr. Edward E. David, had
assured Florence Mahoney that the bill would not be subject
to a veto even though the feeling in the executive branch
was that a "disease of the month" was not a sound approach
to health research and that NICHD was doing an adequate job
on aging. He said the president would sign the bill
because it had passed the Congress and the chance of an

override would be "bad politics" even though the thinking
of the White House was that older people were "not a very
effective lobby."[14] It would be good for the president's
image, and the actual dollars to be expended were relatively
low.

Springer had gone to the White House to make sure that
nothing would happen to the bill, and Nixon told the
distinguished and influential Republican that he did not
see any problem with it at all.[15] Although Rogers had
shepherded the bill through the House, it was still known
as "The Springer Bill." Naturally, Congressman Springer
was shocked to learn that the bill had not been signed.

On the same day, Nixon refused to sign another bill on
behalf of the elderly--the Older Americans Comprehensive
Service Amendments of 1972 (H.R. 15657). The two pocket
vetoes came at the close of a presidential campaign by an
extremely confident incumbent--in a few days he would be
reelected by a landslide.

Apparently gerontology research was judged not to have the
vote-getting power of income maintenance and health care
benefits.

When the institute bill and the Older Americans Amendments
arrived on the president's desk, a third bill affecting the
elderly, the Social Security Amendment of 1972 (H.R. 1),
was already there. This was the bill hailed by the administration on many occasions, including the 1971 White House
Conference and at hearings on the institute bill, as
containing so many benefits for the elderly. As expected,
the president signed H.R. 1. In his statement accompanying
the signing of H.R. 1 into law, President Nixon said that
the legislation "represents another step in my effort to
end the gap that separates far too many older Americans
from the mainstream of American life" and this bill "sup-
ports my conviction that the best way to help people in
need is not with a vast array of bureaucratic services, but
by providing them money and insurance so that they can
secureneeded services themselves. The president concluded:
"I am highly gratified to be able, at long last, to put my
signature on H.R. 1--thus lifting these long-sought benefits
out of debate and placing them into the laws of our generous
and compassionate land."[16]

With all three bills on his desk at one time, circumstances
gave a seasoned politician a unique opportunity to do some
political balancing. In his Memorandum of Disapproval, the
president stated that "Although I support some of the goals
of these two bills, careful review has persuaded me that

neither bill provides the best means of achieving these goals. Both authorize unbudgeted and excessive expenditures and would also require duplications or fragmentations of effort which would actually impair our efforts to serve older Americans more effectively. I have decided therefore to withhold my approval from these two pieces of legislation."[17]

The president also noted that the secretary of DHEW had appointed a new Technical Advisory Committee for Aging Research (TACAR) to "develop a plan for bringing together all the resources available to the Federal Government in the aging research field."[18] The first meeting of that group had been held on October 10, just a few days before the president's veto.

The Nixon veto appears to have been based on logic and astute political sensitivity. Even the most ardent gerontologist agreed that the aging process begins early in life and that aging research should be in the broader context of research on life-span processes. Thus, a new institute would not only duplicate activities already authorized at the National Institute of Child Health and Human Development, but it would also fragment those efforts and increase administrative costs. To this argument Nixon added that TACAR would develop the comprehensive coordinated program of aging research which he felt was needed. The implication in his earlier message to Congress that research ranges all the way from "biomedical to transportation systems analysis, from psychology and sociology to management science and economics" was that the research area and the problems were too broad to be encompassed in a single institute. He objected to the provision of a new grant program for mental health facilities for the aging because it duplicated the "more general flexible"[19] authorities contained in the Community Mental Health Centers Act. The veto rationale was good, but more importantly the president balanced his refusal to approve this legislation with the signing of H.R. 1 on the same day, which he described as "landmark legislation that will end many old inequities and provide a new uniform system of well-earned benefits for older Americans...many improvements and expansions of the Social Security, Medicare, and Medicaid programs...."[20] The president knew where the votes were and what the real concerns of the people were.

The same day the president expressed his disapproval of H.R. 14424 to the House of Representatives, his press secretary, Ron Ziegler, was saying that "no one here at the White House directed activities involving sabotage, spying and espionage"[21] at the Watergate. The Watergate scandal that followed would disrupt the Congress and delay later action to legislate an institute on aging. On November 7, Nixon and Agnew were reelected with 66.8% of the popular vote and 97% of the electoral vote.

Whatever the president's motives, supporters of the bill were stunned with the news of the disapproval. Springer reported that "Florence Mahoney was flabbergasted with the veto" and that when his staff called him at home and told him that Nixon vetoed it, he "couldn't believe it. Of course, you never go back to the President and say why in the hell did you do that. What you had I'm sure with that staff down there was a whole lot of economy going on at this particular point and this was one of the easy ones to get out so he just vetoed the bill."[22] Springer pointed out that Nixon was not risking anything politically. He was overwhelmingly favored in the election and "the Republican party had already lost a big group of the elderly because the Democrats had put into operation so many programs for older people."[23] In Springer's speculation, the president took the position that, "if NIH doesn't want it why do we need it. Legislation is explained in general terms to a President and he gets some picture, but he doesn't get very much of an intimate picture."[24] Springer felt his surprise all the more because he knew that Nixon's parents had gone through problems similar to his: "Nixon went through some very difficult personal circumstances with his aged parents, but you find people have gone through such a struggle and say, well I made it, they can make it, and Nixon has a little bit of that feeling."[25]

James Murphy, former counsel on the Senate Subcommittee on Aging, felt that "the veto reflects more than anything else the supreme self-confidence of Nixon's people in October 1972, when McGovern was obviously floundering, the Republican candidates were far, far ahead and felt they could do whatever they wanted to and did not have to be particularly concerned about the aging constituency to the extent that there was one. The National Council of Senior Citizens was working actively against Nixon at that time anyway and the others, the American Association of Retired Persons and the National Retired Teachers Association, always had had a somewhat more Republican slant, although I think in 1972 they were fairly outspoken against Nixon as well."[26]

According to former NIH Director Marston, the reason for the veto "was probably spending--the Nixon Administration was interested in containment and simplification of government. There was almost an automatic reaction that anything new was to be vetoed with the main purpose being to cut back."[27]

The president had received mixed signals from his adminis-tration's agencies. NIH had prepared a veto message and officials there felt strongly that the bill should be vetoed, but the higher levels of HEW recommended approval, arguing that the bill had wide public and congressional support and that a veto might be construed as an indication that the problems of older people did not rank high in the administration's priorities. Both the Office of Management and Budget and the Office of Science and Technology disap-proved of the bill. To all the arguments against the bill already expressed by NIH, the Office of Management and Budget added that it "could raise false expectations that the aging process can somehow be controlled and managed through biomedical research.[28] The old skepticism about aging research was still alive.

NOTES

1. Richard Nixon, Making Recommendations for Action on Behalf of Older Americans, House of Representatives document No. 92-268, 92nd Congress, 2nd Session, March 23, 1972, p. 24.

2. Rodney H. Brady, memo to the secretary, April 5, 1972.

3. E. O. 11007, February 26, 1962, prescribes the method for formation and use of public advisory committees.

4. Elliot Richardson, news release, U.S. Department of HEW, Office of the Secretary, June 6, 1972.

5. Elliot L. Richardson, "Remarks to Members of the Technical Advisory Committee on Aging Research," minutes of the meeting of October 10, 1976.

6. Frank Church Developments in Aging: 1971 and January-March 1972, a Report of the Special Committee on Aging Persuant to S. Res. 27, Senate 92nd Congress, 2nd Session, Report No. 92-784, May 5, 1972, p. 73.

7. Robert Marston interview, May 14, 1978.

8. F. Marrot Sinex, interview, July 25, 1978.

9. John F. Sherman, interview, June 14, 1978.

10. John F. Sherman, memo to Search Committee, August 22, 1972.

11. Congressional Record-Senate, 92nd Congress, 2nd Session, October 12, 1972, pp. 35407-35408.

12. Glenn Beall, C.R., October 12, 1972, p. 35408.

13. Thomas Eagleton, C.R., October 12, 1972, p. 35408.

14. Edward E. David, interview, May 17, 1978.

15. William Springer, interview, June 13, 1978.

16. Richard Nixon, "Statement by the President on Signing H.R. 1 into law. October 30, 1972," Weekly Compilation of Presidential Documents, 8 (November 6, 1972): 1602-1603.

17. Richard Nixon, "The President's Memorandum of Disapproval to Two Bills Concerning Programs for the Elderly. October 30, 1972," Weekly Compilation, p. 1604. Though dated October 30, 1972, in the Compilation, the "Memorandum of Disapproval" appeared in the Congressional Record on October 18, 1972, p. 37202.

18. Ibid., p. 1605.

19. Ibid.

20. Nixon, Statement on H.R. 1, p. 1602.

21. Ron Ziegler, in Richard M. Nixon, the White House Transcripts (New York: Bantam, 1974).

22. Springer, interview, June 13, 1978.

23. Ibid.

24. Ibid.

25. Ibid.

26. James Murphy, interview, May 10, 1978.

27. Marston, interview, May 14, 1978.

28. Memorandum for the President, October 22, 1972, OMS files, p.4.

III
Establishing an Institute

9
A Second Passage

The 92nd Congress had no opportunity to override the president's veto. The only way for the institute bill to become law was for the 93rd Congress to repeat the entire process of introducing bills in the House and Senate, holding hearings, voting, and submitting a passed bill to the president for signature. To strengthen the new bill, Congress was careful to respond to the president's objections regarding the provision for Community Mental Health Centers and the purpose of TACAR. However, history also contributed to making the bill's course certain. During the year the bill was in the legislative process, Congress was engrossed in the many events of Watergate. Senator Erwin's Committee request for the White House tapes had been rejected. On October 23 of that year, forty-four Watergate-related bills were introduced in the House, twenty-two calling for impeachment of the president or for an investigation of impeachment proceedings. Watergate engulfed the Congress, and the bill to create a National Institute on Aging got little attention from the White House.

With passage of the bill more or less assured, witnesses at the second round of hearings allowed a smoldering dispute —the conflict of biomedical and social sciences research mandates—to become somewhat fiery. Furthermore, exchange between the subcommittee members and the administration's witnesses were more pointed and their relationships seemed

more stressful, as though nerves were frayed and tempers
short as a result of the need to be going over the same
ground covered in previous hearings.

COUNTERING OBJECTIONS TO THE BILL

In the first session of the 93rd Congress, Senator Eagleton
introduced the Research on Aging Act of 1973 (S. 775) and
Congressman Rogers introduced a companion bill (H.R. 65) in
the House. Eagleton's Research on Aging Act called for the
same institute and was nearly identical to the bill (H.R.
14424) passed by the 92nd Congress. A minor difference in
the bills was that the proposed institute became referred
to as the National Institute on Aging rather than the
National Institute of Aging.

The one major change was that the mental health provision
for the aged was deleted because the Community Mental Health
Centers legislation was itself up for renewal that year and
would include the provision, cited by the president as a
reason for vetoing H.R. 14424. Acknowledging the president's objections, Eagleton commented that "While I am
convinced that the President's veto was ill-advised...I do
not believe that this concession to his views will detract
from the primary purpose of this bill--to expand biological
and psychosocial research into the aging process."[1] Testimony in the House and Senate upheld the deletion. In the
House, Rogers pointed out that Congress was accommodating
the president with the deletion.

Eagleton had not forgotten the importance that Nixon in his
veto message and administration witnesses in earlier testimony had ascribed to the functions of TACAR in planning and
coordinating aging research. In introducing his bill,
Eagleton observed that, in the light of Nixon's assertion
that a new institute would duplicate the activity of TACAR,

> This committee was established--perhaps coincidentally
> --at a time when it seemed clear that the Research in
> Aging Act was moving through Congress toward final
> passage....I cannot say with any certainty whether or
> not the establishment of this Technical Advisory Com-
> mittee was merely an effort to head off this legisla-
> tion, to which the Administration previously announced
> its opposition. In any case, I do believe that such a
> committee...can play a major role in developing a
> research plan as directed by this legislation. The
> research itself, however, can only be conducted under
> the auspices of an appropriate body and, for this, I am

convinced that the new Institute on Aging is vitally needed.[2]

At the Senate hearings on the new bill, Eagleton made TACAR's ineffectiveness apparent by asking if the TACAR staff were represented. The administration had to respond, "No, there is nobody here."[3] During the House hearings, Sinex took a swipe at TACAR, which, he said, has "not a single biologist or physician on this committee. Is this the committee which is going to initiate the national biomedical plan?"[4]

HEARINGS ON THE NEW BILL

Hearings were held in March 1973, but the bill was not passed by the Congress until May 1974. This time the delay was on the House side. The Senate passed its version of the bill on July 9, 1973, but the House version did not pass until May of the following year because of the Watergate events.

The House held hearings on the Research on Aging Act (H.R. 65) on March 16, 1973, eleven days before the Senate's hearing on March 27, 1973. Essentially, the positions of all parties at these hearings were the same as they had been earlier; few new arguments were brought to bear. The administration took its traditional position, and the dispute about biomedical and social sciences research intensified.

The Administration's Position

The administration's witnesses this time around were HEW Undersecretary Frank Carlucci, accompanied by Dr. John S. Zapp, deputy assistant secretary for legislation, DHEW; Dr. John F. Sherman, acting director of NIH; and Dr. Gerald D. LaVeck, director of NICHD. Nothing had changed in the administration's position. The undersecretary, as lead-off witness, and Sherman, in answer to questions, reiterated the Department's objections. First, a new institute was unnecessary and would duplicate the work and legislative authority of NICHD. Second, the statutory requirement for an aging research plan was unnecessary because TACAR would fulfill that responsibility. Third, the political impact of diseases should not be the determining influence of funding, especially when scientific leads were lacking. Carlucci reminded Congress that it had created NICHD and that it was not giving the institute adequate time to do its job and be evaluated. Arguing that new institutes are duplicative and hamper intellectual exchange, he pointed out that in the 92nd Congress, more than 100 bills for particular diseases were introduced and that, had these been enacted, they would have split up research teams; fragmented existing, well-integrated programs; and added more personnel to the federal payroll.[5]

During the Senate hearings, after listening to a recitation of the familiar administration opposition, Eagleton asked Sherman if "these same objections with respect to overlap, duplication, administrative costs and so forth" were not raised at the time Congress created the Eye Institute. Sherman replied that Senator Eagleton would recall that the NIH had opposed the creation of that Institute for those same reasons, but now, four or five years later, he had "no hesitation in saying that the quality of that work is first rate. Our responsibility is, once given by an Act passed by the Congress and a bill signed by the President, to do the best job we can in the way of resources."[6]

Dispute about Biomedical and Social Sciences Research

The issue of biomedical versus social sciences research raised its head again in both hearings, this time with a stronger tone. The conflict was articulated primarily by Dr. Denham Harman, president of the American Aging Association, and Dr. F. Marott Sinex.

Harman told the House subcommittee that the social and behavioral aspects of aging should not be the concern of the new institute: "...if I had to put research on the social and behavioral aspects of aging and the biomedical problem of finding practical means of slowing up the aging process and increasing the years of healthy life, on a priority scale of 1 to 1,000, I would put the social and behavioral work at 1 and the biomedical studies at 1,000."[7]

Harman began his Senate testimony by explaining about the aging process and the possibility of pursuing biomedical research leads that might result in significant increases in average life expectancy with concomitant increases in the period of healthy life:

> The problem of finding practical means of slowing the aging process is far too important to permit the new Institute to engage in activities that do not directly relate to this goal....

The sociological, psychological, and economic problems
of the aged are an important concern of society but
actions relating to that concern should not be a
responsibility of the National Institute of aging, but
of an organization such as the Administration on
Aging....By concentrating the effects of the Institute
on this important basic biological problem, there will
be a much better chance of having practical means of
slowing the aging process available in the relatively
near future and with them prospects for more years of
healthy useful life.[8]

Harman strongly recommended that the bill to establish NIA
be modified to limit its mandate to biomedical research.
He would not have the institute engage in training activities because he believed that young scientists would come
into the aging field through biomedical aging research
projects.

Harman evidently took Eagleton by surprise with his strong,
but late, objection to the inclusion of social science
research. Eagleton turned to Harman's four companions for
a response: "Would any of the previous witnesses wish to
give us a brief response to the major thesis of Dr. Harmon
[sic] so far as restricting the role of the new Institute
of Aging is concerned to biomedical research?"[9]

Sinex, the biochemist who advocated psychosocial research
and had tried to mediate between the two competing factions
of researchers, was quick to take up the cause of the
social scientists as he had in the past. He said, "I do
not think that scientists should quibble that one person's
field is necessarily more important than another. What we
are all trying to do is improve the quality of life of the
elderly and their health."[10] His argument was simply
that social science research was not being done anywhere
else, and that the AoA did not now and, in his view, could
not ever have the capability of managing such research. He
felt that the AoA had no cohesive program of research and
that if the new institute did not take the social scientists, they would have no place to go. He agreed with
Harman on the importance of biomedical research which would
help people live longer, healthier lives, and that such
research would solve many problems of our society, "but it
will also create some other problems, and I think it is
appropriate there be research to deal with this."[11]

Harman retorted:

The problem of finding practical means of slowing up the
aging process is far too important to permit the new

Institute to become entangled with relatively minor problems.

It should be kept in mind that the average life expectancy has increased from 45 years in 1900 to 70 years today, and this has not been accompanied by any overwhelming social and psychological problems.

Changes in life expectancy which are likely to come from biomedical aging research will not come overnight, they will come slowly permitting, as in the past the gradual adjustments that may be needed.

The importance of biomedical aging research is vastly greater than that of social and psychological aging studies. Aging is the major factor that keeps us from living longer and better. These other problems are relatively minor.[12]

Dr. Robert Binstock, professor of politics and social welfare at Brandeis University, also stated the position of the social scientists. He saw NIH as a place where no one is

...developing a program that looks at the impact of biomedical findings upon the nature of society and life for older persons, now and in the future. And there is no one looking at the impact of social trends upon biomedical developments for adults and the aged....."[13]

To the Congress, however, the need to include social issues in the mission of the institute was clear from the testimony of many witnesses in California at the Cranston hearings. The social issues were the ones that the people could understand and support.

Rogers concluded the House hearings on a positive note by again recognizing the presence and contribution of Florence Mahoney, "a vigorous advocate for doing something on this problem of aging."[14]

FROM COMMITTEE TO FLOOR VOTE

Passage by the House

The Research in Aging Act encountered no resistance in the formalities of being passed by the House. Rogers and ten cosponsors introduced a clean bill, H.R. 6175, to the subcommittee on March 27, 1973, with only two technical wording changes. The bill was voted unanimously by voice vote out of subcommittee and reported to the Committee on Interstate and Foreign Commerce. The committee reported H.R. 6175 to the House on March 13, 1974.

During the May 2, 1974, House floor debate, Congressman Claude Pepper (D-FLA) spoke first in favor of the new institute. Such support came as no surprise since Pepper, a senior citizen himself, had long been interested in aging matters.[15]

During debate on the House floor, one last attempt was made to accentuate biomedical research on the aging process within the proposed institute. Representative John Y. McCollister (R-NEB) rose to ask the chairman if he might engage "in colloquy" with Congressman Rogers and Dr. Tim Lee Carter of the Health Subcommittee. McCollister stated that he understood that emphasis would be given to biomedical aspects of the aging process as opposed to the social and behavioral research, and quickly added that he certainly hoped that it would. Carter was not sure about his answer, but responded, "I believe that it does. In fact, it is mentioned more often. I believe it is mentioned twice. But the emphasis, of course, should be on biomedical to determine the cause of aging, as I see it...." This did not satisfy McCollister and he turned to Rogers, "Would the gentleman from Florida agree?" Rogers was more positive: "Yes. I think definitely we want the biological research carried on. I think we addressed this on page 5 of the report saying that emphasis is on biological research, although we have given this authority where it has some significance, so I think the real thrust of this bill is the biological research."[16]

The text of the report, however, is worded in such a way that a social scientist could certainly construe a different interpretation of the intent:

> It should be emphasized that the new Institute's mandate includes behavioral, as well as biomedical, research. Many of the problems associated with old age can be approached by the social scientist or the psychiatrist, even though they may also involve questions relating to physical health....This authority for research on the psychological, social, and behavioral aspects of aging is not meant to diminish present or future research on the biology of aging. Such research must be expanded but this should be done in the larger research context authorized by the bill.[17]

Toward the close of the House floor debate, the elderly H. R. Gross (R-IA), who could always be counted on for a conservative, negative word, provided a light note: "I would like the attention of our distinguished Speaker to point out to him that this bill also offers help to those in middle life, as well as the aging like myself." After being told he was a little late with that proposition, Gross continued, "Give me a little help on this, Mr. Chairman. What will this do for me and the others like me, us old geezers, by way of social uplift as mentioned in the bill?"

Rogers: "The major thrust of the bill is for research of a biological nature."

Gross: When the gentleman gets to be 75, he will not be thinking in terms of certain biological matters; but go ahead."

Rogers: "There are other biological purposes than the gentleman may be referring to, for instance, the aging process." With that, Rogers proceeded with a serious effort to persuade Gross.

Gross concluded with an opinion on the bill: "I do not think this bill can do much harm. I do not think it can do much good. If the Members will be reasonable in the future--I will not be here when they start putting money into it--maybe somebody will get a little good out of this new Institute, this new bureaucracy the Members are establishing allegedly for the benefit for the aging."[18]

Congressman Tennyson Guyer (R-OH), then ended the day with a rhyme: "I believe this definition might help to climax the very pleasant dialogue we have heard here on the floor of the House today. The quotation I have in mind is as follows:

> A man is not old when his hair turns gray,
> Nor is he old when his teeth decay,
> But he is certainly headed for the last long sleep
> When his mind makes plans his body can't keep."[19]

Two speakers called for an overwhelming House vote in order to evidence sufficient support for the measure to prevent it from being vetoed again by the president as in 1972. In the voting, 379 answered "yea," 1 "nay," 2 "present"; 51 were recorded as "not voting."[20]

Passage by the Senate

As in the House, the Senate bill encountered no barriers on its way to becoming legislation. The Subcommittee on Aging considered S. 775 in an executive session on May 10, 1973, and reported it with a technical amendment to the Committee on Labor and Public Welfare. On June 5, 1973, the committee ordered that it be reported with amendments to the Senate. On July 9, 1973, the Senate unanimously passed the bill by voice vote.

THE FINAL VERSION

Apart from the technical process of formally substituting the language and number of the Senate bill for the House bill, no compromises or accommodations were required in arriving at the final version of the Research on Aging Act of 1973 (S. 775).

During the Senate vote on the final version, May 16, 1974, Senator Glen Beall again spoke in favor of the bill. Pointing out the decrease in funding for aging research between 1974 (almost $16 million) and 1975 (almost $14 million), he said, "...I believe that this budget cut demonstrates once again the need to increase the visibility and effectiveness of aging research at NIH. The director of a separate institute on aging would have the institutional position to fight his or her own budget battles within NIH, HEW, or OMB."[21] Beall said he had written to the chairman and ranking minority member of the Appropriations Committees urging restoration of the $2.1 million reduction. He then asked for permission to print in the record the text of the letter he sent to President Nixon urging his signature on S. 775.

Eagleton said that it was clear that the "operations of the Technical Advisory Committee on Aging Research over the last 2 years have had no significant impact on the problems that I have described"[22] and then said that he hoped the president would see fit to sign this legislation.

LEGISLATION TO ESTABLISH AN INSTITUTE

With the passage by the Senate on May 16, 1974, a major strategy had been achieved, namely, to get the bill to the president in 1974 in sufficient time to prevent a pocket

veto.[23] This time the bill came to the president's desk
at a time when he no longer had overwhelming confidence
about his popularity with the American people. He was
barraged with calls for impeachment for his involvement in
Watergate, and in a little more than two months he would
resign his post.

Dr. Kretchmer, director of NICHD, remembers that one of his
first duties in 1974 had been to write a veto message for
this bill so that the NIH was prepared for a second
veto.[24] Kretchmer suggests that had Watergate not
occurred, Nixon probably would have vetoed the bill
again.[25] Others agreed with Kretchmer and speculated
that the overwhelming vote for the bill the president had
previously vetoed may have been as much an anti-Nixon vote
as it was pro-aging. Jim Murphy, with staff experience in
the Senate, believes that the changed Nixon position between
1972 and 1974 was not because of the growth or power of an
aging lobby, but was explained by the difference between
how Nixon felt about his own situation: "Since the House
was already engaged in impeachment, this was probably one
of the many things he signed one day and had no idea of
what he was signing. Besides, it was just not a time to
alienate Congress, and the Congress had given Nixon a
little change, 'something to hang their hats on,' by
deleting the mental health provisions to which Nixon had
objected."[26]

On May 31, 1974, President Nixon signed P.L. 93-296
establishing the National Institute on Aging.

                               NOTES

1. Thomas   Eagleton,   Congressional   Record-Senate,   93rd
    Congress, 1st Session, February 6, 1973, p. 2124.

2. Ibid., pp. 2124-2125.

3. Frank C. Carlucci, Research on Aging Act, 1973, Hearing
    on S. 775 before the Subcommittee on Aging of the
    Committee on Labor and Public Welfare, U.S. Senate,
    93rd Congress, 1st Session, March 27, 1973, p. 53.

4. F. Marott Sinex, National Institute of Aging-1973,
    Hearing before the Subcommittee on Public Health and
    Environment of the Committee on Interstate and Foreign
    Commerce, House of Representatives, 93rd Congress, 1st
    Session, on H.R. 65, March 16, 1973 (Washington, D.C.:
    GPO, 1973), p. 64.

5. Carlucci, March 27 Hearing, p. 47-50.

6. Sherman, March 27 Hearing, p. 52.

7. Denham Harman, March 16 Hearing, p. 59.

8. Denham Harman, March 27 Hearing, pp. 59, 60.

9. Eagleton, March 27 Hearing, p. 64.

10. Sinex, March 16 Hearing, p. 64.

11. Sinex, March 27 Hearing, p. 65.

12. Harman, March 27 Hearing, p. 65-66.

13. Robert Binstock, March 27 Hearing, p. 41.

14. Paul Rogers, March 16 Hearing, p. 69.

15. He voiced one of his aspirations: "I have hoped that
    we could set up in the House a special, either select
    or legislative, committee dealing with the problems of
    the elderly. I am disappointed that such a committee
    has not been recommended by the Select Committee on
    Committees....I am going to continue to fight for such
    a committee." In 1977 Congressman Pepper became
    chairman of the House Select Committee on Aging and
    also chaired its Subcommittee on Health and Long-Term
    Care. Congressional Record-House, May 2, 1974, p.
    H3505.

16. John Y. McCollister, Tim Lee Carter, and Carl Rogers,
    Congressional Record-Extensions of Remarks, May 6,
    1974, p. E2759, reporting on May 2, 1974, House of
    Representatives.

17. Research on Aging Act of 1974, Report No. 93-906 on
    H.R. 6175, House of Representatives, 93rd Congress,
    2nd Session, March 13, 1974, p. 5.

18. H. R. Gross and Carl Rogers, March 13, 1974, pp.
    3511-3512.

19. Guyer, March 13, 1974, p. 3513.

20. The "nay" was voiced by Congressman Earl Landgrebe
    (R-IN). The two "present" (but casting no vote) were
    Congressman Gross and Congressman Goodeing (R-PA).
    The 51 "not voting" were not present.

21. Glenn Beall, <u>Congressional Record-Senate</u>, 93rd Congress, 2nd Session, May 16, 1974, p. 8270.

22. Eagleton, <u>C.R.</u>, May 16, 1974, p. 8271.

23. James Murphy, interview, May 10, 1978.

24. This time officials in the Office of the Secretary agreed with NIH and recommended a veto, but the Office of Management and Budget revised its earlier position and now recommended approval on the grounds that the bill contained no provisions for funding but "...merely provides a new and more visible organization to conduct ongoing activities. In addition, sustaining a veto would be difficult in view of the considerable congressional and interest group support as reflected in the Senate and House votes." (Memorandum for the President, May 24, 1976, signed by Roy L. Ash, OMB Files, p. 5.)

25. Norman Kretchmer, interview, June 5, 1978.

26. Murphy, May 10, 1978.

10
Implementation
Off to a Slow Start

> ...the mere presence of an issue on the agenda of
> legitimated public responsibilities in no way can be
> taken as a sign that the issue will be resolved.[1]

Advocates of aging research and their ally in Congress, the
Senate Special Committee on Aging, were keeping a close
watch on NIH to see what would become of this new institute
that the administration did not want. They were concerned
about the organizational alternatives NIH officials were
considering for NIA which would give the new institute less
status than the other NIH institutes. Some NIA officials
were even reluctant to see NIH be the lead agency for implementing the legislation. Because the new law had such broad
mandates and required a research plan for all of HEW, they
would prefer that the AoA or the Office of the Secretary of
HEW implement the law. Others felt that NIA need not be
free-standing but should be under the umbrella of some
larger structure with "bureau" status, for example, a
"Bureau of Human Biology" organizationally equal to the
Cancer and Heart Institutes.[2]

A second concern was the level of funding and staffing NIA
would receive at a time when resources were less plentiful
than in the past. The president was calling for a decrease
in federal expenditures and a cutback of 40,000 federal
employees. Social scientists were worried that their
disciplines would not receive an adequate share in the
biomedical research milieu of NIH. The proposed budget for

155

fiscal year 1975 allowed $14.4 million and 179 positions
for the new NIA. In the previous fiscal year, the Aging
Program at NICHD had spent over $17 million, and the Bal-
timore Center had over 150 personnel. Essentially, the
administration was proposing to create the new institute by
simply transferring existing aging program personnel and
providing fewer dollars.

HEARINGS BEFORE THE SENATE SPECIAL COMMITTEE ON AGING

The research advocates turned to the Senate Special
Committee on Aging for help in monitoring NIH to create a
full-fledged, fully funded institute. Just two months
after the NIA law was signed, on August 1, 1974, the
committee held hearings to "make certain that we [the
committee and the administration] are agreed, or substantially in agreement, on administration plans to
implement Public Law 93-296."[3] Senator Lawton Chiles
(D-FLA) presided at the hearings. Testimony at the hearing
was given by some new administrative officials in traditional roles and by some familiar research advocates in new
roles, including Dr. Carl Eisdorfer and Dr. Ewald Busse.

Implementation of the Law and Status of NIA

On July 24, 1979, Senator Chiles sent a letter to the new
NIH director, Dr. Donald S. Fredrickson,[4] requesting
testimony on NIA before his committee. The request was
unusual in that such requests usually are sent to the
secretary of the department, not to an agency chief.
Instead of Fredrickson, Dr. Charles C. Edwards, assistant
secretary for Health, testified at the August 1, 1974
hearings, accompanied by Dr. Ronald Lamont-Havers, deputy
director of NIH and chairman of the NIH Search Committee
for the director of NIA, and Arthur S. Flemming, now
commissioner of the Agency on Aging.

Edwards knew the concerns of the committee and the research
community and was prepared to address them. Bringing the
committee up to date on the administration's plans to
implement P.L. 93-296, Edwards reported that NIH had been
designated the lead agency for implementation of the law,
and that an implementation plan had already been
developed. Various "organizational alternatives" for
location and management of the new institute had been
examined, and a proposal for a separate NIA had been
prepared. An interagency committee would be formed to

implement the law, and coordination would be developed with AoA and the numerous other agencies involved with aging. Flemming confirmed that AoA was working in concert with NIH and would coordinate all efforts with an interdepartmental workgroup on aging and its task force on research. Thus, two of the concerns of the committee and the research advocates were temporarily dismissed; NIH would be the agency to implement the law, and NIA would be organizationally equal to the other ten institutes.

In response to Senator Chiles' query about the plan for a research program required in less than a year, Edwards was extremely confident: "I think we may see this set some records, as a matter of fact, for Government bureaucracy, in terms of time between passage of the law and implementation of the law. I think we are way ahead of schedule...."[5] Though Edwards stated that HEW was hopeful that the act would be fully implemented by December 1, with a director for the institute on board by the end of 1974, it was May 1976 when NIA had a director and December 1976 when the research plan due in May 1975 was presented to Congress.

The complexity of the institute's status in relationship to other national bodies with apparent responsibility for aging research surfaced at the hearings. What would the role of the recently created Federal Council on Aging be in relation to NIA, its Advisory Council, the NIH Interagency Committee, the Cabinet-level Committee on Aging chaired by the secretary of HEW, and its interdepartmental workgroup chaired by Commissioner Flemming? Flemming clarified the roles of the committees and advisory groups. He explained that the Cabinet-level Committee on Aging with its subgroups was a governmental body charged with the responsibility of coordinating the various aging programs among the several departments. The NIA Advisory Council, made up of nongovernment expert advisors, would serve as other NIH councils, to advise the new institute regarding its mandate. The interagency committee, with NIH as the lead agency, would direct the implementation of P.L. 93-296 to ensure that the activities of the new institute were well coordinated with other HEW agencies involved in aging. The new Federal Advisory Council on Aging would report to the president as an oversight body, charged by law to make certain studies and recommendations to the president and Congress regarding the entire field of aging. The membership of the Federal Council, with the exception of the secretary of DHEW and the commissioner of aging, would be persons from outside the government.

Carl Eisdorfer, well known to the committee for years for
his testimony supporting aging research, spoke at these
hearings as the chairman of the Committee on Research,
Development, and Manpower of the new Federal Council on
Aging. Eisdorfer voiced concern that the various committees and councils which Flemming had described would have
overlapping functions and for that very reason fail to
serve their purposes:

> ...often in the past, overlapping between Federal
> agencies has resulted not in an overzealous effort to
> compete, and to do a good job, but withdrawal from the
> area of overlap, to the point where we have a signifi-
> cant gap.
>
> To a certain extent this has been part of the history
> of research in aging. In observing from the outside,
> various Government agencies point a finger at another
> Government agency and say they will let them do it.[6]

Funding

The issues of funding and staffing caused a rallying of
efforts. For the first time, now that the legislation was
passed, the American Geriatrics Society joined the lobby
effort. Although organized in 1942, a few years before the
Gerontological Society, the Geriatrics Society had never
been politically active. The members of the Geriatrics
Society were mostly practicing physicians whose purpose was
to share medical practices and problems. As a group, they
did not advocate research or political movements to better
the lot of the aged generally. Many members of the
Gerontological Society, on the other hand, were not only
social scientists by training, but also social activists by
inclination.

Dr. Ewald Busse, from Duke University, a psychiatrist who
testified earlier in favor of the NIA as the president of
the American Psychiatric Society, was president-elect of
the Geriatrics Society in 1974. Both he and Dr. Robert B.
Greenblatt, then president of the Geriatrics Society,
collaborated with Dr. Ethel Shanas, the new president of
the Gerontological Society, to prepare a joint policy
statement on the NIA. At the hearings, Shanas pointed out
that the proposed budget of $14.4 million was no more than
what was allocated to NICHD for its existing Aging Program.
The two societies took the position that the funding level
for the new institute should be $49.5 million for its first
two years, approximately $25 million for fiscal year 1975.
They asked for 100 additional positions for the new

institute. The Gerontological Society independently submitted for the record a statement on budget and staffing for NIA prepared by F. Marott Sinex.

Biomedical and Psychosocial Research

The old struggle between the biomedical and social scientists continued, but a concerted effort was made to assure inclusion of all types of research. The joint policy recommendation of the Geriatrics and Gerontological Societies was that the director and deputy director should "represent both the biomedical, social and behavioral sciences"[7] and that the scientific members of the National Advisory Council of NIA be balanced to include representatives of medical, social, and behavioral disciplines. Rudolph Danstedt from the National Council of Senior Citizens backed Shanas in her recommendation by suggesting that if the director is a biologist then the deputy director should be a social scientist.

Senator Chiles tried to elicit the administration's views on the questions of emphasis among the competing disciplines and how the law would be implemented in this respect, but Edwards was somewhat evasive:

> It would be presumptuous on my part, when we have an Interagency Committee of real experts in the field.
>
> They are trying to come to grips with this problem. Although I have personal feelings on the matter, I really would hesitate to discuss this balance, on how much will be in the social field, how much in the biomedics field, without first getting recommendations from this group, when it is established, and it will also depend on the feelings of the new Director, and also of the National Advisory Council.[8]

Later, however, Busse responded to the question Senator Chiles had put to Edwards. Using the example of senile dementia as a probable multifactorial disease, he argued that:

> ...we are not only obligated in searching for biological explanations, we are very obligated to look at the social and physical environment to see what adverse forces impinge on the individual. So that, in my viewpoint, as the new Institute emerges, it will be very shortsighted not to recognize, as we move in the basic science of aging, how we can relate organic changes, social stress, and how the individual functions in

society. Hostile features in the environment can be
altered to reduce the adverse manifestations of many
diseases.[9]

Walter Beattie, president of the Association for Gerontology in Higher Education, joined Busse in his multidisciplinary view of the aging process and suggested even
broader responsibilities for the new institute:

> ...I would like to underscore...the need to involve a
> broad range of disciplines such as economics, political
> science, anthropology, and those beyond the more typical
> psychological and sociological orientation. Of primary
> importance is a multidisciplinary approach which will
> promote interdisciplinary research and training where
> appropriate. It would also be my view that the Insti-
> tute should be organized around the functions it will
> carry out. Hopefully, these will include but not be
> necessarily limited to: (a) Biomedical research and
> training; (b) behavioral-social science, research
> training; (c) evaluative and impact research and
> training; and (d) public information and education.[10]

Beattie further made an appeal for multidisciplinary centers
to be supported by NIA.

Other groups continued the theme in other types of demands.
The National Council of Senior Citizens wanted applied
research to be the emphasis of the institute. The National
Caucus on the Black Aged recommended that NIA have a
Section on Black Aging headed up by an associate or deputy
director, and that NIA provide graduate and postgraduate
training programs in all fields related to aging.

A more excluding note was introduced by Dr. Bernard
Strehler, president of the Association for the Advancement
of Aging Research. Although not asked to testify at the
hearings, Strehler submitted a detailed plan for implementing P.L. 93-296 which included a list of physicians and
biomedical scientists as nominees for the NIA directorship.
Strehler commented that he knew of no behavioral or social
scientists "whose expertise extends sufficiently into the
biomedical area" to be qualified for the job.[11]

The new institute would have to be all things to all elderly
and their advocates. Eisdorfer observed that "...we have to
be very careful that having gotten the NIA through its ene-
mies, that it not be smothered by its friends, by saddling
it with too many peripheral or conflicting roles which it

could not possibly handle."[12] What would be the future of this new institute with such a broad mandate that almost every group interested in aging could see a different role for it, an institute as yet without a director, staff, or start-up funding?

WAITING FOR THE RESEARCH PLAN

One month after the August 1 hearing, NIH officials could see that they were not ahead of schedule for establishing a National Advisory Council on Aging. Nor was it likely that a research plan could be developed by May 31, 1975. Dr. Norman Kretchmer, director of NICHD and acting director of NIA, and his assistant James G. Hill, met with Rogers' and Eagleton's staffs to negotiate for more time to complete the plan required by Congress. Rogers' staff refused to accept the NIA proposal that an "outline" of a plan be submitted by the May 1975 deadline with the full plan to follow at a later date. NIA called the May deadline an "unreasonable time constraint" but Rogers' staff urged that efforts be made to comply with the law and indicated that Rogers would be sending a query to Secretary of HEW Weinberger asking for information about NIA developments and strongly criticizing HEW for delays in the formation of a National Advisory Council on Aging.

Eagleton's aide, James J. Murphy, was somewhat more understanding and, although he would not say that development of the plan could be delayed, he indicated that the senator would be willing to discuss problems in the development of the plan when they actually occurred. Murphy even offered to put pressure on the HEW secretary's office if it would help to speed the establishment of the National Advisory Council on Aging. The plan was not submitted until December 1976.

THE LONG SEARCH FOR A DIRECTOR

It is regrettable that the world's largest research center has been politicized. The morale continues to decline and finding qualified replacements for those who leave is becoming harder and harder. Indeed, the NIH has been without a full-time Director for nearly 4 months. I hope that rumors that a Director will be named today are true. I also hope that the administration will appoint an Assistant Secretary of Health, and fill the vacancies which exist at two of the Institutes now.[13]

These words of Congressman Rogers opened the hearings before
the House Subcommittee on Health and the Environment on
April 21, 1975; the subject was an oversight of NIH. A
year had passed since the signing of the NIA Act, but the
institute was still without a director. It was a time of
no leadership. Marston left NIH in January 1973 just
before the Watergate scandal broke.[14] It was four months
before his successor, Dr. Robert S. Stone, appointed by
President Nixon, became the tenth NIH director. Stone did
not stay long; an academic administrator, he was not popular
with the biomedical research community. NIH had a series
of acting directors. The lack of a single, strong leader
and the unsettled nature of the times politically may have
been a factor in the slow selection of a director for NIA.

Consideration of a director for NIA had actually begun
before the law was passed by Congress the first time. Even
as NIH officials were writing a veto message for the bill,
other NIH officials were preparing for implementation of
the law. The first meeting of a search committee, chaired
by Dr. John F. Sherman, deputy director of NIH, was held on
August 15, 1972, to organize the effort of securing names
for consideration of the directorship of NIA. Defining the
program scope of the institute was a prerequisite to setting
up criteria for candidates; thus, at that first meeting
considerable discussion was about the nature of aging
research and the probable program scope of the new institute. The group tentatively agreed that the program of the
new institute would include both behavioral and biomedical
aspects of aging research, but that the NIH should resist
efforts to sponsor service programs such as those at NIMH.

Florence Mahoney was involved in the selection process at
this early and later stages. Before the meeting, Sherman
called her to ask for her recommendations of individuals to
consider for the directorship. She gave him the names of
biomedical researchers she felt were qualified, and named
others whom she felt would better serve the new effort by
continuing their own research rather than becoming director
of the new institute.[15]

The preparations for a search effort were short-circuited
by the president's veto of the bill and by possibility of a
veto the second time around. NIH took no serious steps to
search for a director until the law was signed, and it was
July 11, 1974, before a search committee was formally
appointed by Stone. Dr. Lamont-Havers chaired the group.
At the August hearing of the Senate Special Committee on
Aging, Dr. Edwards, assistant secretary for Health, had
assured the committee that NIA would have a director by the

end of 1974.   It was October 1974 before the Search
Committee began to interview candidates for the job.

Announcements in Science, the New York Times, and other
publications produced applications from nearly seventy
possible candidates from many disciplines.   The committee
scheduled interviews in October and November with five of
those applicants they felt were highly qualified candidates.[16] The leading candidates turned the position down
because the salary level and security NIH offered could not
compete with their academic appointments.   At one point the
committee thought the position was filled.   It appeared
that a well-known microbiologist from Stanford University
would take the position, but a dispute arose over the
ownership of cell tissues developed by him under an NIH
grant.   The controversy caused the candidate to withdraw
his name from consideration.   Thus, in May 1975, one year
after the legislation was passed, the acting director of
NIH explained before the House Appropriations Committee
their difficulty in filling the position of director of
NIA.   The post had been offered to eight individuals, all
of whom felt the salary of $36,000 fell far short of their
needs.

Florence Mahoney followed the problems of recruiting a
director for NIA with frustration and disappointment.   The
individuals she had recommended had turned down the job
offer, and others NIH did not wish to consider.   She and
NIH officials had been seeking a biomedical scientist for
the post, but as time went by and no suitable biomedical
research candidates seemed willing to take on the job, she
began to consider other possibilities.   Dr. Robert N.
Butler was a practicing clinical psychiatrist and gerontologist who also had experience as a researcher at the
National Institute of Mental Health.   Although his name was
on an early list of possible candidates for the position,
he had not been considered as a candidate, probably because
of the biomedical focus of the search efforts.   Mrs. Mahoney
read his Pulitzer Prize winning book, Why Survive? Being
Old in America, phoned him, and asked him to meet with her
at lunch.   Busy with other commitments, she forgot the
lunch appointment, but dropped everything to meet with
Butler later the same day.   Highly impressed with Butler's
wide range of interests and knowledge, she felt he was a
potential director for the new institute.   The next day she
called Dr. Theodore Cooper, then assistant secretary for
Health, and later Dr. Don Fredrickson, the new director of
NIH, and Dr. Ronald Lamont-Havers, chairman of the search
committee, to say that she had talked with Butler and that
he "is absolutely sensational."[17]   Why couldn't he take

on this job that nobody wanted? She believed he would be
willing to do it. Butler also had the backing of an
influential HEW insider, Arthur Flemming. All agreed to
consider Butler as a candidate and he became director of
NIA on May 1, 1976.

THE STRUGGLE FOR FUNDING

Advocates of aging research knew that the battle for support
of aging research was not won with the passage of the bill
which mandated an institute at NIH. On the last day of
hearings on the bill to create NIA, Marott Sinex, who had
been testifying in favor of increased federal funding for
aging research since 1967, concluded his remarks with a
note of concern about the future:

> The quality, quantity and impact of research on aging
> is dependent on the passage of this legislation. We
> may have to bide our time for money and effective
> Administration implementation. However, now is the
> time to pass the only legislation which can do the job
> of providing better health for the elderly in their
> later years.[18]

Sinex was an academician who learned a great deal about the
politics of health while working with his lobbyist friend,
Florence Mahoney. She continually reminded him of the
importance of the appropriations processes.[19] Congress
ultimately controls what government will do through its
exclusive power to appropriate money, as established in the
Constitution: "No money shall be drawn from the Treasury,
but in consequence of appropriations made by law" (Article
I, Section 9).

Funds would have to be authorized and appropriated, positions allocated, and the law implemented by an agency that
did not want it in the first place. But achieving the goal
of increased federal funding for aging research was still
in doubt. A year earlier, in July 1973, Sinex led a group
of witnesses[20] before the Subcommittee of the Senate Committee on Appropriations to testify regarding appropriations
for the aging program within NICHD. Sinex pointed out that
appropriations for research on aging decreased in the year
of the White House Conference, and he illustrated the type
of problems created by the lack of funds. NIH had solicited
proposals about the failure of immune function in aging and
had received twenty-seven applications; nineteen were
approved by the study sections, but only two were funded
because of lack of money.

Now Congress was allowing a mere transfer of the existing NICHD budget (about $13 million) for aging to the new institute:

> The legislation contains no new authorizations of appropriations. The legislation will require minimal administrative cost for the creation of the mandated new National Institute on Aging and, while the Committee cannot estimate these costs, they should be slight.[21]

In an attempt to counter this short-sighted thinking, Sinex testified as a representative of the Gerontological Society before a Subcommittee of the House Appropriations Committee on May 9, 1974, just one week after the NIA bill had been passed by the House. He pointed out the implications of the level and timing of funding on the potential of the new institute:

> If the administration and the Congress made no response to the National Institute of Aging authorization legislation, funds would eventually be transferred from the aging program of Child Health to the new Institute. The staffing of the new Institute is critical for the development of the program. A director must be selected and a head of intramural and extramural programs appointed. Operating costs would increase by $750,000 or more and these would have to come out of the existing budget. A council must be formed and a program developed. All of this will require some time for deliberation and consultation....If the President signs the National Institute of Aging legislation, and no supplemental appropriation is made it would mean that the new Institute would be making its initial presentation to this committee in May of 1975. The first council approvals under the new Institute's expanded budget would come in June and October of 1975 with the first significant new funding in January 1 of 1976. To those of us who hold high expectations for the new Institute this seems like a very long time indeed. By that time the promise and excitement of the new Institute will seem like a distant yesterday. The members of this committee have the knowledge and ability to expedite an effective program. Is there any way that the new Institute could become a real institute rather than a paper institute without an 18-month delay? During this 18 months you and I and millions of Americans are not getting any younger. An Institute ceases to be a rather poor relative and becomes a real institute when its budget reaches about $30 million a year. An institute dealing with problems as important

as aging should reach $50 million as rapidly as possible.[22]

Sinex recommended that the proposed $13 million budget be increased to $19.6 million. He made the same case before the Senate Appropriations Subcommittee on June 16, 1974, after the bill had been passed and signed.

Persistence for Funding

Florence Mahoney was determined to see NIA funded at a level that would, in her view, be adequate for the first year of its existence. The House Appropriations Committee had allowed only $15.5 million for NIA in fiscal year 1976, no more than the budget for 1975.[23] This time she called on Representative Gilbert Gude (R-MD), member of the House Select Committee on Aging, to introduce from the floor of the House an amendment to the NIH appropriations bill. Gude had expressed interest in the aging research issue and Florence felt that bipartisan support would strengthen the appeal. She convinced Gude that the appropriations for NIA should be almost double. Surprisingly, the administration agreed with her. Dr. Norman Kretchmer, director of NICHD and acting director for NIA, had testified that NIA needed $32 million to get off the ground.

On the evening of June 25, 1975, when the NIH appropriations came up for a vote, Gude offered an amendment which would increase the NIA appropriations from $15,526,000 to $29,500,000. He reported the NIH officials had told him that the proposed $15.5 million budget would neither expand the existing research program nor support staff for the new institute which had only five staff members at that time. Congressman Gude ended his argument for additional funds by urging his colleagues to be foresighted and seize the opportunity to attack the problems of aging before it was too late: "Lets [sic] not have hundreds and hundreds of warehouses full of old people not in command of their wits and senses. Lets [sic] find ways to keep our senior citizens hale and hardy in their old age."[24]

Representatives Paul Rogers, William Randall (D-MO), and Bella Abzug (D-NY), all spoke in favor of the amendment, but Congressman Daniel J. Flood (D-PA), chairman of the Appropriations Subcommittee on Departments of Labor and Health, Education, and Welfare strongly opposed it. Accepting amendments would open the bill to more amendments and make it vulnerable to a veto, and here was a Republican asking to double the budget. Flood compared his colleagues to "special pleaders" and pointed out the contradiction in the plea to balance the budget yet fund everyone's special interest or project. His main objection to additional funds for NIA was that it was premature. The institute was not eight months old; it had no permanent director and no signs of getting one in the near future. Worst of all, NIA had not fulfilled its obligation to Congress to submit a research plan by May 31, 1975:

> What is the first thing Congress said to the Institute? "You must have a comprehensive plan for aging research. Before you get a dime, you must have a comprehensive plan for aging research." Congress said: "You just submit that plan by May 31 of 1975."

> All right here we are tonight, June 25, 1975. There ain't no plan. We have no idea--neither do they--when they are going to submit it. They told us that. These are very honest people; no director, no plan, no address, no nothing; and we gave them $15 million.[25]

Three members of Flood's subcommittee took the floor to concur with his opposition to the additional funds.[26] The most persuasive argument against the amendment was developed by Congressman David Obey (D-WIS). He professed to be very much in favor of funding the institute, but he was afraid that if the dollar amount of the appropriations bill got too high it would be vetoed. He reminded his colleagues that the Congress recently had been unable to override five fairly important vetoes by President Ford. In view of the fact that Congress had not received the required comprehensive research plan which would explain how the money would be spent, why not wait and, if the plan should appear, the funding could be added to the Senate bill. As an afterthought Obey added that he considered it a mistake to compartmentalize research areas and that it would probably be wiser to increase funds at the Institute of General Medical Sciences as a means of helping the study of the problems of aging.

Robert Michel (R-ILL) likewise opposed the amendment and took a direct swipe at Gude:

> ...the gentleman [Gude] voted for a $30 million increase a few minutes ago and now he wants a $15 million increase here. He also wants a few million for the subway. We cannot have it all that many ways. The gentleman is all for these nice-sounding programs, but we cannot afford all these things. Very little of it comes to play in Peoria.[27]

The proposed amendment was rejected: ayes 27, noes 83.
Gude demanded a division and a recorded vote, but a
recorded vote was refused. The appropriations for NIA for
fiscal year 1976 remained at $15.5 million.

NIA TODAY

Early implementation of the NIA legislation was not expedi-
tious. Almost a year passed before the first meeting of
the National Advisory Council on Aging required under the
law, and it took two years to recruit a director for the
institute. Although NIA had been legally established by a
formal statement published in the Federal Register on
October 7, 1974, it was not until a council had been formed
and a director appointed that the new institute really
began to function as a separate entity.

The law creating NIA required a research plan to coordinate
and promote research into the biological, medical, psychological, social, educational, and economic aspects of aging
by May 1975. It was December 1976 before that plan, entitled "Our Future Selves," was transmitted to Congress.
That plan provides only broad guidelines and general
directions to be pursued; thus the federal government still
does not have a comprehensive, coordinated, operational
research plan. The efficacy of the new institute in promoting research on all aspects of aging remains unknown,
but the present status of NIA in terms of funding, staffing,
and early directions provides some clues to the future.

NIA Budgets

Four years of fiscal data are not enough to project future
growth of the new institute. Nevertheless, available
information gives some indication of NIA's early growth
trends in comparison to the ongoing growth trends of other
institutes and NIH as a whole.

NIA is no longer the smallest institute in terms of research
actually funded or research applications received.[28] The
institute received its first independent budget in 1976,
and from 1976 to 1980 the total institute budget more than
tripled. By 1979, not only had the total budget tripled,
but also research grants almost tripled, contracts almost
doubled, and training increased to about what it had been
at NICHD. The total budget is approaching the amount recommended ($75-90 million) for 1981 by the institute's research
plan (see Table 10-1).

Table 10-1. Aging Program Budgets and NICHD and NIA
Budgets[a] (in thousands of dollars)

Fiscal year	Total budget[b] (aging program)	Research grants	Research contracts	Training
NICHD 1968	68,621 (7,973)	3,503	213	2,197
NICHD 1969	73,126 (8,268)	3,485	325	2,286
NICHD 1970	70,095 (8,100)	3,226	458	2,314
NICHD 1971	94,760 (9,313)	3,801	240	2,232
NICHD 1972	116,427 (12,505)	5,756	907	2,104
NICHD 1973	130,429 (12,650)	6,169	691	1,522
NICHD 1974[c]	125,455 (17,203)	9,230	765	2,572
NICHD 1975	142,435 (15,989)	7,753	605	1,812
NIA 1976[d]	19,288	10,023	838	1,750
NIA 1977	30,000	17,652	1,823	2,193
NIA 1978	37,305	21,955	1,979	2,385
NIA 1979	56,911	37,211	3,493	2,378
NIA 1980	69,988	43,328	6,194	2,776
NIA 1981	76,091	47,589	5,769	2,598

[a] Sources: "National Institute on Aging, Development of
the 1979 Appropriation" NIA Budget Office Document;
"National Institute on Aging, Obligations for Aging" NIA
Budget Office Document; "National Institute of Child
Health and Human Development, Historical Analysis by
Program FY 1964-1979" NIA Budget Office Document; Basic
Data Relating to the National Institutes of Health,
1979, Office of Program Planning and Evaluation and the
Division of Research grants, NIH, 1979.

[b] Total budget includes research grants, contracts,
training funds, intramural research, and administrative
costs.

[c] The 1974 budget for aging includes $1,445,000 impounded
funds.

[d] In FY 1976 the federal government changed over from a
fiscal year beginning on July 1 to a fiscal year beginning October 1. Therefore, the 1976 budget represents
a 15-month fiscal year. Amount shown is for 12 of the
15 months.

A perspective on this apparently substantial increase in funding at NIA is gleaned from the context of budget increases at other institutes and at NIH as a whole. Between 1976 and 1979, the total NIH funding for research grants doubled, from $263 million to $525 million.[29] In relationship to NICHD, whose budget for research grants doubled from $19.9 million in 1976 to $40.9 million in 1979, the 1979 NIA funding would represent 28% of the NICHD grant funding were the programs still combined in the same institute, double the highest portion of the budget (14% in 1974) ever allowed the aging program at NICHD through 1975.

NIA's budget has quintupled from $14 million in 1976 to $70 million in 1980. Grant applications more than quadrupled from less than 200 in 1976 to over 800 in 1979, with more than half of those funded. Compared to the billion dollar budget of the National Cancer Institute, the largest institute at NIH, the NIA budget and staff seem tiny. On the other hand, like other institutes, NIA has steadily grown since its creation, and it is no longer the smallest institute, having surpassed two others in funds. NIA seems to be keeping pace with NIH as a whole in terms of fiscal growth, and aging research is faring somewhat better than it did in terms of funds allocated during the NICHD years, even with additional administrative costs of a separate institute.

Staffing. Funds are essential to an institute's survival, but staffing is equally crucial for program development and management. Growth in staff must be commensurate with the increase in funding for efficient and prudent use of those increases. NIA staff positions, though few, have had an increase in budgeted positions, with the largest number each year in the area of intramural research. Table 10-2* puts NIA staffing in perspective with the largest institutes, the National Cancer Institute and the National Heart, Lung, and Blood Institute, and another new and small institute, the National Eye Institute (NEI). Clearly, NIA and NEI have only a fraction of the staff that the larger institutes use to maintain their programs. Gerontologists complain about the few, overworked staff at NIA and would like to see the interests of each discipline better represented in the institute's staffing pattern.

Categories of Research. Each year the number of research grant applications received by NIA has increased, as has the number of applications approved. The number of grant applications received for all categories increased from less than 200 in fiscal year 1976 to over 800 in fiscal year 1979. Each year the biological category has received

*For Table 10-2, see pp. 172-173.

by far the most grant applications, more than half. The biological category had by far the largest percentage of grant applications approved as well (Table 10-3*).[30]

When biological and clinical grant applications are combined, the predominance of the biomedical field is even more evident. Yet, if the membership categories of the Gerontological Society are an accurate reflection of the percentages of gerontologists in various interest areas, the great majority of gerontologists are behavioral and social scientists.[31] The old grievance of the behavioral and social scientists that the research milieu of NIH does not encourage social research would seem more valid if the number of applications they submitted were higher. Consistently during 1978-1979, they submitted less than half as many applications as the biological category alone received. Whatever the reason, biomedical research substantially outweighs behavioral and social research support by NIA.

NOTES

1. Robert H. Binstock, "Federal Policy Toward the Aging-- Its Inadequacies and Its Politics," The Economics of Aging, a National Journal Issues Book (Washington, D.C.: The Government Research Corporation, 1978), p. 57.

2. James Hill and Joel Hedetniemi, memo to Norman Kretchmer, June 21, 1974.

3. Lawton Chiles, Establishing a National Institute on Aging, Hearing before the Special Committee on Aging, United States Senate, 93rd Congress, 2nd Session, August 1, 1974 (Washington, D.C.: Government Printing Office, 1975), p. 2.

4. Fredrickson replaced Dr. Robert Stone who had been appointed by Nixon in May 1973 when Marston left office.

5. Charles C. Edwards, August 1 hearing, p. 5.

6. Carl Eisdorfer, August 1 hearing, p. 22.

7. Ethel Shanas, August 1 hearing, p. 12.

8. Edwards, August 1 hearing, p. 5.

9. Ewald W. Busse, August 1 hearing, p. 11.

*For Table 10-3, see pp. 172-173.

Table 10-2. Selected NIH Staffing[a]

	Fiscal Year 1977			Fiscal Year 1978		
	No. on board 9/30/76	Budget positions	Ceiling	No. on board 9/30	Budget positions	Ceiling	No. on board 9/30
NCI	1926	2029	1954	1955	2040	2040	1961
NHLBI[b]	748	747	719	723	773	773	770
NIA	181	200	194	191	223	227	223
NEI	129	152	146	143	171	171	156

[a] Source: NIH, Position/Employment Ceiling Allowance versus On-Board Permanent Full Time Employment, NIA Budget Office Documents.

[b] Source: Budget Office, NHLBI, telephone conversation, March 1, 1980.

[c] NIH ceilings are now based on full-time equivalent work years.

Table 10-3. Research Project Grant Applications by Category, NIA

	1976			1977			1978		
	No. recv'd	No. aprvd.	Aprvl. rate (%)	No. recv'd	No. aprvd.	Aprvl. rate (%)	No. recv'd	No. aprvd.	Aprvl. rate (%)
Biological	135	90	67	213	138	65	238	167	70
Clinical	20	7	37	27	13	48	60	29	49
Behavioral	56	25	45	64	30	47	51	23	45
Social	16	6	40	22	9	41	76	30	39
Total	225	128	57	326	190	58	425	249	59

Source: NIA Budget Office, National Institutes of Health.

Fiscal Year 1979			Fiscal Year 1980			Fiscal Year 1981		
Budget positions	Ceiling	No. on board 9/30	Budget positions	Ceiling	No. on board 9/30	Budget positions	FTE[c] Ceiling	No. on board 9/30
2058	1915	1963	2058	1961	1837	2065	1962	
786	733	736	771	744	771	771	671	
258	232	242	303	277	242	305	254	
186	169	168	178	178	168	178	152	

1979			1980			1981		
No. recv'd	No. aprvd.	Aprvl. rate (%)	No. recv'd	No. aprvd.	Aprvl. rate (%)	No. recv'd	No. aprvd.	Aprvl. rate (%)
424	297	70	391	293	75	420	329	78
110	55	50	58	33	56	84	55	65
95	44	46	77	42	55	122	68	56
102	24	24	115	38	33	137	45	33
731	420	58	641	406	63	764	497	65

10. Walter M. Beattie, August 1 hearing, p. 17.

11. Bernard L. Strehler, August 1 hearing, p. 55.

12. Eisdorfer, August 1 hearing, p. 23.

13. Paul Rogers, Committee on Interstate and Foreign
     Commerce, Hearings before the Subcommittee on Health
     and the Environment on Legislative Oversight on the
     NIH, House of Representatives, 94th Congress, 1st
     Session, April 21, 1975 (Washington, D.C.: Government
     Printing Office, 1975), p. 1.

14. Immediately after his reelection in November 1972,
     President Nixon requested the resignation of 2,000
     senior government officials. Dr. Robert Q. Marston,
     director of NIH and leading administration witness at
     the Senate hearings, was not among them because he was
     not a "Schedule C" appointee.

     Rather, he was asked if he would like to assume some
     federal position other than director of NIH. Marston's
     response was no. He left NIH in January of 1973 amidst
     an enormous outcry of protests from the academic and
     biomedical research community that President Nixon had
     "politicized" the NIH directorship. Six months later,
     in May 1973, Dr. Robert S. Stone replaced Marston, only
     to be fired a year and a half later, in January of
     1975. His successor, Dr. Donald S. Frederickson, was
     appointed six months later. Meanwhile the NIH deputy
     director and the deputy director for science resigned
     soon after Marston left.

15. John F. Sherman, memo to acting director of NIH,
     August 22, 1972.

16. Dr. Leonard Hayflick, Stanford University; Dr. Carl
     Eisdorfer, University of Washington; Dr. James E.
     Birren, University of Southern California; Dr. Ewald
     Busse, Duke University; Dr. Edwin Bierman, VA Hospital,
     Seattle, Washington. From memo October 11, 1974,
     Ronald Lamont-Havers to Search Committee.

17. Florence Mahoney, interview May 15, 1979.

18. F. Marrot Sinex, Research on Aging Act, 1973 Hearings
     on S. 775 before the Subcommittee on Aging of the Com-
     mittee on Labor and Public Welfare, 93rd Congress, 1st
     Session, March 27, 1973, p. 20.

19. Florence Mahoney had learned about the difference between authorization and appropriation the hard way with the National Mental Health Act of 1946. See Strickland, Politics, p. 46.

20. Dr. Adrian Ostfeld of Yale University; John Martin, former commissioner of Aging; and William Hutton, executive director of the National Council of Senior Citizens.

21. Research on Aging Act of 1974, Report No. 93-906 to accompany H.R. 6175, Committee on Interstate and Foreign Commerce, House of Representatives, 93rd Congress, 2nd Session, March 13, 1974, p. 2.

22. Sinex, Hearings before the Subcommittee of the Committee on Appropriation, House of Representatives, 93rd Congress, 2nd Session, May 9, 1974, pp. 300-301.

23. The exact amount was $15,526,000 for FY 75 and an additional $3,943,000 for the period from July 1, 1973 to September 30, 1976. This interim funding was due to the change in the beginning of the fiscal year from July 1 to October 1.

24. Gilbert Gude, Congressional Record, House, June 25, 1975, p. 20847.

25. Daniel Flood, C.R., June 25, 1975, p. 20847.

26. Representatives Neal Smith (D-IA), Robert H. Michel (R-ILL), David R. Obey (D-WIS).

27. Robert Michel, C.R., June 25, 1975, p. 20849.

28. From 1968 through 1975, NIH aging research grants, contracts, and training grants were funded by the National Institute of Child Health and Human Development. From 1968 to 1971, the aging budgets at NICHD changed little. In 1972, grants and contracts received large increases and by 1974 had almost tripled over 1968. For all years, training funds stayed about the same or decreased, an NIH-wide trend. Despite increases in dollars for aging research at NICHD, the aging budget never exceeded 14% of the total NICHD budget. (See Table 10-1).

29. The total NIH budget increased 50%, from $2.3 billion to $3.2 billion. Grant funding by NCI and NHLBI, the

two largest institutes, increased only 62% and 58%, respectively, during the same period. In 1979, research dollars for NIA grants were double those for the National Institute of Environmental Health Sciences (NIEHS) and the National Institute for Dental Research (NIDR), although the three small institutes were very close in grant funding until 1978.

30. More than the numbers of grants awarded in each category, the research priorities for each program area might be an indication of the direction aging research is taking. Program announcements for biomedical and clinical research grants from 1976 to 1980 solicited research on the genetics of aging, especially cellular models; the metabolism and reactions of the aged to drugs; diabetes and related problems; immune function and age-related effects; nutrition and aging, especially effects of obesity and health maintenance; and models for aging of the muscles and bones. Program announcements in social and behavioral research emphasized sociocultural factors among minority groups, the impact of retirement and bereavement on aging, and the relationships of the aging process to social and historical change.

31. As of March 1980, the membership of the Gerontological Society was divided as follows: Biological Sciences, 429; Clinical Medicine, 762; Behavioral and Social Sciences, 2,197; Social Research Planning and Practice, 1,198; Members-at-large, 290.

11
NIA and Aging Research
Political and Scientific Bases
of Research Policy

The plural forces which struggled for and against the establishment of the National Institute on Aging largely determined its present nature. Scientific inquiry into biomedical research issues and concern about an increasing elderly population stimulated interest in the beginning. The multidisciplinary nature of gerontology broadened that interest and gave it impetus. Changing social attitudes and issues surrounding the elderly gave significance to research on aging, as did the growth of age-based organizations, the increasing demands for health services for the elderly (such as Community Mental Health Centers), and the recognition politicians gave to the potential of gray power.

Forces opposing the creation of an institute were equally strong and persist today. NIA was established despite a political climate that opposed a fragmentation of research programs and a proliferation of institutes at NIH, and despite congressional concern about the "disease of the month club" approach to biomedical research. The legislative and implementation processes for the institute occurred during a Republican administration which was pushing to decrease federal spending and to cut back on the number of federal employees. The success of the NIA campaign in the

face of these odds is in part attributable to the fact that
aging was a research area with four decades of increasing
momentum harnessed and directed by skilled and determined
individuals and groups at every essential political phase.

A résumé of these combating forces and their strategies in
the framework of agenda-building provides a context for
interpreting the events which ultimately created the institute and which could influence its future development. A
long and slow prelegislative process in which scientific
and social issues interacted and merged led to the policy
decision to create a separate institute for aging research.
That process corresponds to the "outside initiative" model
of agenda-building used by political scientists to explain
how an issue arises in nongovernment groups, then expands
to the public agenda and the formal agenda of Congress.[1]
According to the model, an issue passes through four major
phases in the agenda-building process: initiation, specification, expansion, and entrance. An issue typically
arises in small groups which begin to expand awareness of
the issue. Occasionally, an issue is redefined in the process of that expansion, usually taking on a more general
meaning.

The early cadre of researchers who perceived support for
research on aging as an issue was small indeed. Even
later, the researchers and advocates from outside the
government who were intent on influencing Congress to
provide more support for aging research were few and had or
used little in the way of resources to achieve their aims.
In the development of a policy for aging research, the
expansion phase was crucial in creating enough pressure and
interest to attract the attention of the Congress. The
uneasy and very loose coalition that the small group eventually formed with other researchers and advocates for the
aged did, in fact, redefine the issue and, consequently,
the mission of the institute which became their strategic
demand. The most critical year and event in the expansion
of the issue were 1971 and the second White House Conference
on Aging. At that time, a convergence of forces and demands
occurred. The Gerontological Society, aged-based interest
groups, a powerful individual catalyst, and public awareness
of the needs of an aging population, united in reiterating
a decade-old demand for a national institute of aging.

Once the issue entered the legislative arena in 1972, the
outsiders who fostered aging research sought the support of
groups and institutions interested in the problems of and
services for the elderly. During hearings on the bill,
these diverse interests influenced the broadened scope of

the institute--almost preventing its creation. An examination of the institutions and actors involved in the course
of events reveals how their separate roles related to the
decision to create an institute and impinged on health
policy development.

The Lobbyists

In discussing the role of the powerful Lasker Lobby in the
making of medical research policy, Stephen P. Strickland
comments:

> For a quarter of a century, a small handful of individ-
> uals outside government have had more to do with final
> decisions about particular medical research policy
> decisions than most of the other participants in the
> policy process whose names appear in the public record
> as science administrators, health officials, or members
> of congressional committees. The unfortunate implica-
> tion of this state of affairs is <u>not</u> that politics
> sometimes dictates medical-research priorities. It is,
> rather, that government science and health officials
> --and presidents and members of Congress--have permit-
> ted the process by which health and science policy
> decisions are made to become a consistently laggard and
> reactive one.[2]

The story of NIA is clearly another case of a few individuals outside of government prevailing in the political
process and influencing biomedical research policy, but
this small group differs substantially from the group to
which Strickland refers. Florence Mahoney, her friends,
and the few leaders from the Gerontological Society were
not a well-financed, carefully organized lobby with
full-time, paid, professional lobbyists. They made no
significant financial contributions to the senators and
representatives they approached for support of the bill.
They did not use the mass media to convince the public that
biomedical research on aging should be a priority of the
federal government.

<u>An Individual Catalyst</u>. When Florence Mahoney lobbied for
an institute for aging research, she did not have available
to her the resources she was accustomed to when she worked
with the Lasker Lobby, nor did she choose to use the same
political style. What Florence Mahoney and Mary Lasker had
in common were charm, intelligence, energy, strong convic-
tions, interest in biomedical research, connections in the
Democratic party system, and access to the gatekeepers of

Congress.   In the case of NIA, Florence Mahoney acted on
her own, and tailored her strategy to the times and needs.
For example, although she and Mary Lasker had been on
friendly terms with President and Lady Bird Johnson and
other Democratic presidents, a Republican president was in
office during the early 1970's.[3]   Mrs. Mahoney knew,
therefore, that she had to go to the Congress to get support for an institute bill.

To influence congressmen, Mrs. Mahoney did not use philan-
thropy to further the cause of aging research, nor did she
make substantial contributions to the campaigns of congressmen likely to go along with her ideas.   In contrast, the
Albert and Mary Lasker Foundation "...created a special
Public Service Award as a judicious means for rewarding
both legislative-and-executive-branch officials who had
assisted medical research.   Hill and Fogarty each received
this award in 1959."[4]   Mrs. Mahoney's style, rather, was
an intensive effort to personally call on senators and
representatives and their staff members to explain the
cause for aging research.[5]   She had to build new working
relationships based on trust once her friends from the
Lasker days, Senator Hill and Congressman Fogarty, were
gone.   She relied on a few non-scientist close friends,
such as Paul Glenn and Lucius Birch, scientists such as
Marott Sinex, and young medical students to help her
behind-the-scenes efforts to persuade Congress.   She never
called on the Gerontological Society nor used it in the way
that Mary Lasker so effectively used the American Cancer
Society.   One reason was that she did not perceive the small
professional group as able lobbyists and, more importantly,
she disagreed strongly with their interest in broadening
the scope of the institute to include social and behavioral
sciences.   She felt that biomedical research was appropriate
for an NIH institute and that social research could be supported by AoA.   She recruited biomedical scientists to talk
informally with congressmen and to testify at hearings on
the bill.

Florence Mahoney's efforts did not extend to the general
public.   She did not use the extensive public relations
resources of the media and "blue ribbon panels" of committed
experts that had often contributed to the success of the
Lasker Lobby.[6]   It was not that she did not have access
to the press and other news media or that she did not have
the skills to use these tools; rather, she felt that they
could be of little help to her in the campaign for research
on aging because "the general public just didn't know what
gerontology was."[7]   Furthermore, aging did not have the
dramatic appeal of the dread diseases such as cancer,
stroke, and heart attack.

Florence Mahoney was an individual catalyst who used personal, "one-to-one," informal lobby techniques. In doing
so, she was no less thorough and effective than she had been
while working with the well-organized, well-financed Lasker
Lobby.

Professional Groups as Lobbyists for Aging Research. In
some regards, Florence Mahoney was correct in her assess-
ment of the ineffectiveness of the Gerontological Society
as a lobby group. Although the organization had long advocated private and public support for aging research, its
membership consisted of only a few thousand researchers and
practitioners, not seasoned lobbyists. The society had no
large full-time professional staff comparable to the American Medical Association or the Association of American
Medical Colleges to represent them in Washington. In fact,
the organization itself was based in St. Louis, Missouri,
until 1970 when its leaders (much to the concern of some of
its members) decided that it was time to move to Washington
"where the action was."[8] Those who objected were afraid
that the professional image of the society would be damaged
and that somehow they would be "corrupted from Potomac
fever." Earlier, the National Retired Teachers Association
had offered free office space to the Gerontological Society
in its Washington office but the society decided not to
accept the offer because it wanted to remain independent of
other age-based organizations; the society was still struggling to establish its professional status within the scientific community. Even after moving to Washington, Edwin
Kaskowitz, the executive director of the society, did not
feel that he "had a clear mandate to lobby."[9] Early
attempts at coalition building in Washington with age-based
organizations such as National Council on Aging, the
NARP/NRTA, and the American Nursing Home Association failed
because each of these organizations was diverted by individual efforts to prepare for the 1971 White House Conference.

During the period of lobbying for the institute bill, the
society still had the atmosphere of a club. Its leaders
came from a few key members referred to as the "old guard,"
usually individual scientists who were the most active in
the cause of aging research. Kaskowitz remembers a "pioneer
feeling" at that time. Staff support for the society was
so small that the officers assumed many responsibilities,
often at their own expense.

Kaskowitz never appeared on the Hill in a formal or informal way to lobby for the institute. He received news of
Florence Mahoney's activities from her friend Marott Sinex,
but he never spoke to her directly.[10] Individual members
of the society always spoke in formal testimony on behalf

of the society, using the society's name, but they were
dedicated individuals, not a well-organized lobbying effort.
In fact, society members expressed their own views when they
differed with those of the officers; for example, Denham
Harman was a strong advocate for an institute exclusively
for biomedical research. Members who were practitioners
advocated more action and less research. Thus, the lobbying
effort of the Gerontological Society was by a few individual
scientists holding leadership posts within the society.

The Congress

In the 1950's and 1960's, Senator Lister Hill and Congressman John Fogarty provided strong leadership within Congress
to favor not only biomedical research in general but also
aging research.[11] However, the Hill-Fogarty leadership
ended before outsiders advocating aging research had reached
the point of demanding an institute. New converts to the
cause of aging research had to be found within the Congress
at a time when the odds were against an easy conversion.
Not only had the Golden Years of support for biomedical
research ended when aging research advocates began to
demand an institute, but also the Congress had a strong
feeling against the disease-of-the-month club approach to
biomedical research. Key congressmen were besieged almost
daily with requests to establish an institute for this or
that, often rare, disease suffered by constituents. Numerous pseudo-agenda bills to create institutes, similar to
the Springer bill, were circulating around Congress with
little or no support.

On the other hand, the cost of Medicare and Medicaid was
already a concern of many legislators working with a fiscal-
ly conservative Republican administration. Also, the social
and political ramifications of an increasingly older population were pressing. Florence Mahoney's persuasive and
timely reasoning with the legislators was that 5% of the
elderly population was in nursing homes at a cost of $11
billion annually and that biomedical research could help
prevent old age disabilities and save taxpayers money.

By the time NIA was on the congressional agenda, senior
citizens had an institutionalized advocate in the Senate in
the form of the Special Committee on Aging, chaired by
Senator Harrison Williams until 1971 when he became chairman
of the Senate Committee on Labor and Public Welfare. Also
in 1971, Senator Eagleton became chairman of the Subcommittee on Aging of the Committee of Labor and Public Welfare.

Although aging research did not have the visibility of other pressing social concerns of the elderly, the members and staff of the Senate Special Committee on Aging had been educated by gerontologists about the possibilities for breakthroughs in research. Williams was willing to introduce his bill and to support the institute concept. Eagleton overcame his early concerns about proliferation of institutes and both he and Paul Rogers were persuaded by Florence Mahoney to introduce institute bills. These and other new advocates, such as Senator Cranston and Representative Staggers, stimulated in part by the education they received from an individual advocate, her colleagues, and a few scientists, brought about the legislation for an institute. The bill had important bipartisan support. Representative Springer, a leading Republican, endorsed the bill because of a personal conviction of its worth. Senator Beall, the ranking minority member of the Senate Committee on Labor and Public Welfare, not only resisted the administration's efforts to convince him to oppose the bill but also became an advocate of the bill. Nevertheless, the strength of Hill and Fogarty was missed in the crucial appropriations area. The bill was passed without authorization of new funds and later attempts to get supplemental appropriations for the institute failed.

The House of Representatives had no committee comparable to the Senate Special Committee on Aging until after the law to create an institute was passed. The House Select Committee on Aging was created as a watchdog over legislative initiatives for the elderly, and since 1975 aging and NIA have had strong backing from that committee under the chairmanship of Mrs. Mahoney's old friend, Claude Pepper.

The President

The increasing visibility of a large elderly population and the collective effort of the coalition of age-based interest groups no doubt influenced Congress to support the institute bill, but the expansion of the issue to accommodate all those interests almost killed the institute before it came into being. The add-on to the bill to include mental health centers was cited as the principal rationale for the president's veto. The provision was deleted later and Congress passed the bill a second time during a period of strong anti-Nixon feelings and Watergate. From the late 1950's on, when the needs of the elderly were just beginning to be expressed, the push for White House Conferences on Aging came from the Congress, not the White House. President

John F. Kennedy had his own research agenda, but it was for
children, not the elderly. Richard M. Nixon, in the role
of president, was without question opposed to the creation
of an institute. As a fiscal conservative, he could see no
merit in adding to the research bureaucracy and expanding
more funds, especially for overhead costs.

Even when the presidents were aware of the aging population
as a social issue, aging research did not have a priority.
Funding for Medicare and Medicaid, national health insurance, and cancer and heart research were the issues of wide
public concern that attracted the attention of the presidents. Research on aging simply was not seen as a major
national issue.

The Research Bureaucracy

From the beginning, the National Institutes of Health resisted a separate institute for aging research, a recognized
conservatism:

> Most Government research agencies, including NIH, are
> characteristically conservative about the kinds of
> science they will support. This stems in part from a
> reaction to the activist role that some research sup-
> porters--including members of Congress and disease-
> oriented lobby groups--have employed, and in part it
> reflects the inherent conservatism of scientific
> establishments.[12]

From a management point of view, NIH argued against duplication of administrative services and costs and against
proliferation of institutes. NIA was the last institute to
come into existence at NIH. From a scientific point of
view, NIH was skeptical of the possibilities of breakthroughs in understanding the complex aging process. Only
a few individuals within the bureaucracy such as Shock,
Parran, Birren, and Butler saw research opportunities in
the field of aging and were prepared to embrace a multidisciplinary approach. Furthermore, the agency already had
a "life process" institute, NICHD. The logical argument
was that many diseases of the elderly are rooted in the
social, physical, and nutritional environment of childhood
and adulthood. To break senescence away from the process
of human development was not rational.

The Greater Scientific Community

The established scientific community and its organizations had a perspective and position on aging research similar to that of the research bureaucracy. In general, the traditional scientists were conservative. Biomedical researchers had a categorical disease orientation and perceived the social sciences as related to social issues, not to health or biomedical research. Scientists distinguished between research on the aging process and research they considered to be "research on behalf of the aged."[13] Gerontologists were unsuccessful in attempts to neutralize this opposition. The competition for funding from NIH and the probability that funds for research on aging would divert funds from other established areas intensified the opposition from the scientific community at large.

CHANGING ROLES

Those individuals and institutions which prevailed in the political process and those who acceded to their demands assumed new and different roles as the issue progressed. Those who pushed for aging research played and exchanged the roles of political catalysts, facilitators, advocates, lobbyists, educators, gatekeepers, and experts. Their own careers developed in relationship to the career of the aging research issue. Opposing forces from within the administration and from biomedical professional groups with competing interests became critics and adversaries.

During the agenda-building process, Florence Mahoney played the role of a political catalyst in approaching and convincing congressmen to introduce a bill to establish an institute. As the issue crossed over into the legislative process, she assumed the role of facilitator-advocate by bringing together scientific experts and politicians and engendering understanding and trust between them. She also served as an educator, training scientists in political tactics and informing politicians about the biomedical subject matter related to the aging issue. During the early implementation of the legislation, Florence Mahoney acted as an unofficial advisor to decision makers in the administration who had the responsibility of establishing NIA. Later she became an official advisor as a member of the first NIA National Advisory Council and continues to be a watchful guardian of that implementation process.

Scientists interested in gerontology were from the beginning the predominant interest group. Researchers such as F. Marott Sinex, Carl Eisdorfer, Bernice Neugarten, Ethel Shanas, Ewald Busse, Bernard Strehler, and Denham Harman became political advocates for the issue of aging research. As their contacts and confidence increased with politicians they, too, became educators of the politicians. They played the same role with their peers, educating one another, training leaders of their professional societies to become lobbyists and witnesses, testifying in favor of aging research and an institute. They involved their organizations as lobby groups and, though diverse and even disputing voices were heard over the need for biomedical research, social science research, and social services, the loud collective voice of these organizations was heard and answered with a single institute and a broad mandate. Scientists and professional organizations who opposed the institute became supporters of the administration's position of nonproliferation. With implementation of the law, the adversaries reassumed their roles as researchers and colleagues.

Finally, several congressmen who initially played the role of gatekeepers to the formal agenda of the Congress became advocates and "experts." As gatekeepers, they were the pivots between the agenda-building and legislative processes, and later between the legislative and implementation processes. Senator Eagleton, who introduced the institute bill, became a strong advocate of aging research. Representative Rogers became not only an advocate but also a thoroughly informed "expert" in the issue of aging research. Senator Cranston, who served on Eagleton's committee, has popularized the issue in articles for the public and is now assuming the roles of advocate and "expert." Senator Percy has recently begun cultivating the role of expert and has written a book on the subject of aging.

Members and staff of the Senate Special Committee on Aging assumed an advocacy role early on in the agenda-building process, as did Congressman Pepper and Congressman Gude in the House when the House Select Committee on Aging began to assume its new role as advocate for the elderly. A different set of legislators, including Senator Magnuson and other members of the House and Senate Appropriations Committees, have a critical role in the funding level for NIA and thereby influence the rate of growth in research possible for the developing institute.

THE CHANGING ISSUES: SOCIAL AND SCIENTIFIC

Not only did the characters and their roles in the NIA process change over the years, but also the social and scientific issues surrounding research on aging have evolved and intensified. The National Institute on Aging was created by the pressing social issues and needs of a growing elderly population rather than by promise of imminent breakthroughs in the area of aging research. Social issues spurred the development of a coalition of age-based groups and bolstered congressional approval. The nature of the demands of elements of the age-based organizations are changing. Gray Power leaders want a major change in society's attitude toward the elderly. These activists see themselves as an untapped resource able to make continuing contributions economically, socially, and politically. Older people do not want to be perceived and studied as a gerontological problem and are articulating their grievances. The elders are beginning to challenge gerontologists in their research and perspective on their "subject."

But without doubt, the increase in the aged population which early gerontologists viewed with alarm has come to pass and the numbers of elderly are still growing. More than 24 million Americans are now over 65[14] --approximately 10% of the population-- and projections indicate that the proportion could double to 20% in the next fifty years.[15] American life expectancy at birth reached 73.2 years in 1977, a gain of 2.3 years since 1970--almost as much of an improvement as occurred between 1950 and 1970.[16]

The economic issues associated with the elderly population boom are now highly visible and considered crucial. Many economic analysts warn that, if the increased population of the elderly materializes as predicted, the effect on health care costs will be staggering. At present, nearly one-third of the $500 billion U.S. budget is spent on the aged, with $90 billion a year for Social Security and about $35 billion for Medicare and Medicaid. The Department of Health and Human Resources projects that, if present trends continue over the next decade, by 1989 about 45% of the federal budget will go to the elderly.[17]

Advocates of an institute for aging pleaded that applied biomedical research could alleviate the economic problem of health care for the elderly, but the basic scientific question of the nature of aging research remains unanswered. In general, the disease-oriented biomedical research community still sees few leads for breakthroughs in the study of the aging process. Scientists today are raising questions about what the consequences of such breakthroughs might mean for society. At least one prominent scientist has called aging research "inopportune" and sees it as "the wrong research on the wrong problem in the wrong era."[18] However, along with an acceptance of an interdisciplinary approach to the study of disease, the vision of early gerontologists is increasing as a more comprehensive understanding of the multiple causes of disease has developed. Emphasis is being placed on the importance of lifestyle, life stresses, nutrition, and other socioeconomic and environmental factors related to health and disease prevention. The emerging holistic approach to health places the individual in the context of all of life's circumstances and implies the need for social science research as well as biomedical research. This parallel development of perspective could reinforce the multidisciplinary nature of gerontology and broaden the study of the life and aging processes.

It is not evident as yet that the institute is the appropriate mechanism to facilitate links between disciplines and encourage the exploration of new paradigms for research. The extramural program of NIA continues to be dominated by the biomedical sciences and at best encourages multiple disciplines. Interdisciplinary research is still an unrealized vision.

IMPLICATIONS FOR RESEARCH POLICY

Today the National Institute on Aging is more symbolic than real. As a symbol, it can be either a unifying principle for diverse groups to further their causes or a meaningless substitute for action. NIA could continue to exist as a mere pacifier for a public that has made and will continue to make demands; it could reenact the role of the old Center for Aging Research, NIH's "paper organization" in the 1940's, of diverting attention by a pretense of action.

NIA is a milestone in the development of gerontology as a scientific discipline and in the definition of aging research. It is the product of the political process and its future will be influenced as much by political forces and social issues as by any advances in science. The institute was a strategy chosen by a small group of lobbyists to attain the goal of improved and increased research on the aging process. This development of an ad hoc strategy by

external forces demonstrates how biomedical research policy
evolves when the federal government fails to take the lead
in developing an overall strategy, not only for research on
aging, but also for all areas of biomedical research.

Aging research remains on the formal agenda of the federal
government, a challenge for the future.

NOTES

1. The two other models are as follows:

    ...the mobilization model, considers issues which are
    initiated inside the government and consequently
    achieve formal agenda status almost automatically.
    Successful implementation of these issues often
    required, however, that they be placed on a public
    agenda as well. The mobilization model accounts for
    the ways decision makers attempt to implement a policy
    by expanding an issue from the formal to the public
    agenda. The third, the inside initiative model,
    describes issues which arise within the governmental
    sphere and whose supporters do not try to expand them
    to the mass public. [From Roger Cobb, J. K. Ross, and
    M. H. Ross, "Agenda Building as a Comparative
    Political Process," The American Political Science
    Review, 70 (March 1976): 127-128.]

2. Stephen P. Strickland, Research and the Health of
    Americans (Lexington, Mass.: D. C. Heath and Co.,
    1978), p. 29.

3. Florence Mahoney, telephone interview, May 5, 1980.

4. Richard A. Rettig, Cancer Crusade (Princeton:
    Princeton University Press, 1977), pp. 26-27.

5. The importance of Ms. Mahoney's lobbying was
    emphasized (often in much detail) in interviews with
    members of Congress and their staff who had worked on
    the NIA legislation, as well as by her advocate
    colleagues and NIH officials who opposed the creation
    of the institute. Not only did all persons interviewed
    who were involved with the NIA legislation spontaneous-
    ly mention the critical nature of the role, but her
    early efforts to get congressional support for research
    on aging in the Veterans Administration were described
    in interviews with government officials of the 1960's.

6. Rettig, p. 41.

7. Mahoney, interview, May 5, 1980.

8. Edwin Kaskowitz, interview, April 27, 1980.

9. Ibid.

10. Kaskowitz did contact Cyril Brickfield of the AARP and
    NARTA in May 1971 to ask for support on two matters of
    concern to the Gerontological Society. One was the
    creation of a Department of Aging within the NICHD and
    the other was restoration of the 10% cutback in
    funding for NICHD. Brickfield noted that the AARP and
    the NARTA had a position of calling for a separate
    institute at the time, but agreed to support the
    request for funding and to talk to Congressman Flood
    and Senator Magnuson. (Memorandum, May 14, 1971, to
    Mr. Bernard E. Nash from Cyril F. Brickfield, AARP
    files.)

11. Hill had a double advantage as a biomedical research
    advocate in the Senate. He took over the chairmanship
    of the Senate Committee on Labor and Welfare in the
    same year that he chose to be chairman of the Health
    Appropriations Subcommittee. It was Florence Mahoney
    who influenced Hill to take the subcommittee post.
    (See Strickland, Politics, pp. 92-94.)

12. Strickland, Research, p. 138.

13. John F. Sherman, telephone conversation, May 9, 1980.

14. Robert J. Samuelson, "Aging America--Who Will Shoulder
    the Growing Burden?" National Journal: A Special
    Report--Growing Old in America, 43 (October 28,
    1978): 1712.

15. Robert N. Butler, "Preface," Why Survive? (New York:
    Harper and Row, 1975), p. xi.

16. Health: United States 1979 (Hyattsville, Md.: Office
    of Health Research, Statistics, and Technology, 1980),
    DHEW Pub. No. (PHS) 80-1232, pp. v, 138.

17. The costs are disproportionate because older patients
    require more physician time, more hospital admissions,
    and longer hospital stays. They are the main users of

long-term care facilities and home health agencies. "Today the elderly are reported to see physicians 50 percent more often, and have twice as many hospital stays that last almost twice as long as is true for younger persons. [From H. Brotman, "The Aging of America: A Demographic Profile, "The Economics of Aging: A National Journal Issue Book, 1979, p. 36]." The Administration on Aging reports that in 1976 older people had about a one in six chance of being hospitalized during a year, whereas the chance for persons under 65 was one in ten (from Administration on Aging, Facts About Older Americans, 1978). The average cost per person over 65 for health expenditures rose from $1,700 in 1975 to $1,745 in 1977 (from New England Journal vol. 297, October 20, 1977, p. 887, and John Iglehart, "The Cost of Keeping the Elderly Well," National Journal, October 28, 1978, p. 1728). In contrast, the average cost in 1977 was $661 for persons 19 to 64 years old and $253 for persons under 19 (Ibid).

18. Robert L. Sinsheimer, "The Presumptions of Science," Daedalus 107, pp. 23-35.

Appendix
Chronology of Events

BUILDING THE AGENDA

1937   Conference on Problems of Ageing held at Woods Hole, Massachusetts, sponsored by the Josiah Macy, Jr. Foundation, the Union of American Biological Societies, and the National Research Council; led to the formation of the Club for Ageing Research.

1938   Publication of <u>Problems of Ageing: Biological and Medical Aspects</u> by Macy Foundation.

1940   NIH conducts survey of research activities in gerontology and establishes Gerontology Research Section at Baltimore City Hospitals with grant from Macy Foundation.

1945   American Gerontological Society organized with Macy Foundation support.

1945   <u>Journal of Gerontology</u> published.

1946   NIH Gerontology Study Section formed in November to review aging proposals.

1948   NIH Gerontology Research Section transferred to National Heart Institute and becomes a branch.

1948   National Institute of Mental Health begins support of research grants in field of aging.

1949   NIH Gerontology Study Section disbanded.

1950   First National Conference on Aging held by Federal Security Agency Recommends National Advisory Council on Gerontology and Geriatrics.

1952   Conference of State Commissions on Aging and Federal Agencies.

1956   Center for Aging Research established in National Heart Institute.

1956   Second Federal-State Conference on Aging.

1957   NIH begins to establish Multidisciplinary Research Centers in Aging.

1959   Edith Green introduces H.R. 3301 86th Congress - 2d Session to establish a National Institute of Geriatrics (January 26).

1961   First White House conference on Aging recommends a National Institute of Gerontology (January 9-12, 1961).

1962   P.L. 87-838 passed, authorizing National Institute of Child Health and Human Development (October 17).

1964   Veterans Administration creates Satellite Laboratory Aging Program.

1965   Gerontology Research Branch at Baltimore becomes part of NICHD and Center for Aging Research becomes Adult Development and Aging Branch.

1965   Older America Act (P.L. 89-73) establishing AoA (July 14).

1966   National Institute of Mental Health established an extramural section on Mental Health of the Aging.

1968   Senator Williams introduces S. 3784, Preliminary Gerontological Research Act.

1969   Senator Williams introduces S. 870, Research on Aging Act.

1969   Richard M. Nixon inaugurated as the 37th president of the United States.

1969   President's Task Force on Aging established (report compiled February 1970).

1969   Rep. Springer introduces H.R. 15158 to establish an institute for biomedical research on aging (December 9, 1969).

1970   Florence Mahoney approaches Yarborough and Eagleton about support of bill for an Institute on Aging.

LEGISLATION FOR AN INSTITUTE

1971 - 92nd Congress - 1st Session

January 22   Rep. Jacobs and three cosponsors introduce H.R. 186 and Bingham introduces identical bill H.R. 601 to establish the Research Commission on Aging --the Research on Aging Act.

January 22   Rep. Jacobs introduces H.R. 188 and six identical bills are introduced to amend the Public Health Service Act to establish a National Institute of Gerontology.

February 2   Rep. Springer introduces H.R. 3335, Research on Aging Act.

February 19   Senator Eagleton and fourteen cosponsors introduce S. 887 on the floor to amend the Public Health Service Act to provide for the establishment of a National Institute of Gerontology.

March 11   S. 887 referred to the Senate Aging Subcommittee.

March 25-31   Joint Senate hearings of Special Committee on
and   Aging and Subcommittee on Aging (of Senate
April 27   Committee on Labor and Public Welfare) to evaluate programs of the AoA and review preparations for 1971 White House Conference.

May 21   Sen. Williams introduces S. 1925, Research on Aging. Calling for an Aging Research

Commission to prepare a long-range program and research plan in all areas.

June 1-2   Senate hearings conducted by the Subcommittee
and 14   on Aging on S. 887, Eagleton bill, and S. 1925.

November 28-   1971 White House Conference on Aging.
December 2

December 14   Roberts and eight cosponsors introduce H.R. 12308 to provide for establishment of a National Institute of Aging (contains mental health provisions but no social science provisions).

1972 - 92nd Congress - 2nd Session

March 3-4   Senate hearings held March 3, San Francisco; March 4, Los Angeles, chaired by Senator Cranston before the Subcommittee on Aging on the following legislation to expand research on aging: S. 887, S. 1925, S. 2934.

March 14-16   House Hearings before the House Subcommittee on Public Health and Environment re: H.R. 12308), H.R. 3335, H.R. 13875, H.R. 8491, and H.R. 11962.

March 23   President sends special message to Congress recommending action on behalf of older Americans; indicates that HEW will create TACAR.

March 30   Amendment 1098 to S. 887 by Cranston, proposes four changes in S. 887 to broaden scope and focus of activities to be carried out by the new institute.

April 5-6   S. 887 considered in executive session by Subcommittee on Aging.

April 17   H.R. 14424 (clean bill) Springer/Rogers; Institute on Aging--Research on Aging Process (also H.R. 14405 Springer bill).

1973 - 93rd Congress - 1st Session

January 3   Rogers introduces H.R. 65 to establish a
               National Institute of Aging.

February 6   Senator Eagleton introduces the Research in
               Aging Act of 1973, S. 775, a bill to amend
               the PHS Act to provide for the establishment
               of NIA within NIH and direct the development
               of a plan for an aging research program.
               Identical to H.R. 1925 and H.R. 14424.

March 16   Hearing on H.R. 65 before the Subcommittee on
               Public Health and the Environment.

March 27   Hearing on S. 775 before Senate Subcommittee
               on Aging.

March 27   Rogers and ten cosponsors introduce H.R. 6175
               as a "clean bill" for H.R. 65.

May 3   Federal Council on Aging established by P.L.
               93-29, Older Americans Comprehensive Services
               Amendments of 1973.

May 10   S. 775 considered in executive session by
               Subcommittee on Aging and ordered reported to
               full committee with a technical amendment.

June 5   S. 775 considered in executive session by
               full committee and ordered reported to Senate
               floor with amendments.

June 30   The Committee on Labor and Public Welfare
               favorably reports S. 775 with technical
               amendments.

July 9   S. 775 passed by Senate with amendment to
               establish NIA within NIH.

July 10   S. 775 referred to House Committee on Inter-
               state and Foreign Commerce.

1974 - 93rd Congress - 2nd Session

March 7   H.R. 6175 Research on Aging Act of 1974
               (legislation similar to H.R. 14424) reported

from the Interstate and Foreign Commerce Committee by unanimous voice vote.

March 13   Committee on Interstate and Foreign Commerce favorably reports H.R. 6175 with amendments.

May 2   House passes S. 775 in lieu of H.R. 6175 amended by inserting language of H.R. 6175.

May 9   House Appropriation Subcommittee hearings include testimony for funds for new NIA.

May 16   Senate concurs with House Amendment to S. 775.

May 31   P.L. 93-296, Research on Aging Act, signed by the president authorizes the establishment of a National Institute on Aging.

ESTABLISHING AN INSTITUTE

1974

July 11   Search Committee for NIA director established at NIH.

August 1   Hearing before the Senate Special Committee on Aging re recommendations for implementation of P.L. 93-296.

October 7   Formal statement of organizational functions and delegations of authority for the NIA published in the Federal Register.

October 13 Federal Council on Aging holds hearings on research on aging.

December 2 NIA General Program Announcement published in the Federal Register.

December 30 Charter for the National Advisory Council on Aging approved.

1975

January 8   The Implementation Plan for P.L. 93-296 submitted to the assistant secretary for Health.

April 23, 24 First meeting of National Advisory Council on
              Aging.

May 31   Research Plan mandated by Congress.

June 25   Request for supplemental funds for NIA
              opposed and defeated.

June 30   Dr. Richard C. Greulick appointed acting
              director, NIA.

July 1   Dr. Donald L. Frederickson sworn in as 11th
              director of NIH.

                            1976

May 1   Dr. Robert Butler becomes director of NIA.

December 8   HEW aging research plan, Our Future Selves,
              required by P.L. 93-296 transmitted to
              Congress.

Index